THE PROMISE OF POWER

POWER

By DeWitt S. Osgood

Southern Publishing Association, Nashville, Tennessee

PREFACE

Let thanksgiving and praise be offered to the Father of lights, and His Son, my Saviour, and to the Eternal Spirit, by whom I have so often been "strengthened with might . . . in the inner man . . . to comprehend [some glimmerings of] . . . the love of Christ, which passeth knowledge." (Ephesians 3: 16-19.)

The Holy Bible constitutes the fountain from which to draw the water of life, but many "able ministers . . . of the spirit" (2 Corinthians 3:6) and Spirit-filled laymen have encouraged me to write this book. In fact, I have gathered materials just about everywhere from speakers, teachers, authors, and dedicated worshipers. This book is my way of sharing with others the blessings of the Spirit that have been shared with me.

I must mention some who have in various ways been most helpful: R. A. Anderson, A. E. Axelson, Theodore Carcich, N. R. Dower, B. P. Hoffman, Mr. and Mrs. Ernest W. Mackie, W. G. C. Murdoch, Arthur L. White, and Sebert G. White.

DeWitt S. Osgood

DEDICATION

In grateful appreciation of the unnumbered blessings that they have added to my Christian experience, this volume is dedicated to my wife, Margaret, and our children, Charlotte, DeWitt Jr., Gordon, Margaret, and Betty Sue.

CONTENTS

Born of the Spirit

Before the Judean hills echoed the joyful strains of angel choirs, before the wondering shepherds sought the Bethlehem stable, before the Wise Men from the East brought their gifts of gold, frankincense, and myrrh, even before the existence of our world, the eternal Son of God decided to be born into the human family. In the councils of heaven before God created man, our Lord made the decision in which the Father concurred (Zechariah 6:13) to restore peace to the universe. To do this He had to tabernacle in the flesh as one with us. Thus He became "Emmanuel," which means "God with us."

Why did the Majesty of heaven leave the ivory palaces? (Psalm 45:8.) Why did He promise to come and enter the body which God had prepared for Him? (Psalm 40:7; Hebrews 10:5.) He Himself gives the answer, "I am come that they might have life, and that they might have it more abundantly." John 10:10. Thus Jesus, the preexistent one, voluntarily chose to be born as a man that He might bring life to us.

But what choice have we in deciding whether we shall come into the world and whether we shall leave it? There is a reason for our entering the world as we do. How could God allow man a choice as to whether to be born without first giving him some kind of existence? How could a man choose unless he first be a free moral agent? How could he choose without knowing what kind of life God offered him? God has given us an existence so that we may decide whether we want to be born again. In our present existence God gives us the opportunity to decide our destiny, be it life or death. The teachings of Jesus and their fulfillment in His life demonstrate the kind of life God offers to all. Man has been given the power of choice. Those who want the only kind of life that will continue forever will have to choose to be born again. He who refuses the rebirth forfeits eternal life. He chooses death.

Christ sacrificed His past at Bethlehem, where He became a man. We are to sacrifice our past at Calvary. At the place of death to "self" we receive the life of Christ. He who dies to sin at the cross inherits the life Christ there bequeathed to us. God even gives man the opportunity to live in this world as he would live in heaven. If after he has tasted the joys of the life to come he feels he doesn't want that kind of life, he can reverse his decision. (Hebrews 6:4-6; 11:15.) Such is the absolute fairness of God.

Just as Jesus in His preexistence was a free moral agent, so man in his present existence is a free moral agent. Christ *voluntarily* chose to be born into the human family. You, too, are free to choose. God will not compel you; He will not force you.

How could the Son of God also be the Son of man? The Incarnation holds mysteries that can never be solved in this life, nor need they be. Some truths we must accept by faith. Nevertheless, we should try to understand as much as possible about the Incarnation. Nearly all know the circumstances of our Lord's Incarnation. To the virgin Mary at Nazareth the angel Gabriel came with the message, "The Holy Ghost shall come upon thee, and the power of the Highest shall overshadow thee: therefore also that holy thing which shall be born of thee shall be called the Son of God." Luke 1:35. And the angel of the Lord told Joseph in a dream, "That which is conceived in her is of the Holy Ghost." Matthew 1:20.

Just as Jesus was born of the Holy Spirit into the human family, so we may be born of the same Holy Spirit into God's spiritual family. Many teachers in the Israel of today are like Nicodemus of old. They are ignorant concerning the new birth. They have an idea that men and women may become new crea-

9

tures in Christ by education, by training, by church membership, or by their own efforts to obey the law. But there can be no new life without the re-creative presence of the "Spirit of life." (Romans 8:2.) Only life can produce life, and the Holy Spirit is not only the "Spirit of life," but the "Spirit is life." (Romans 8:10.) Christ's night-school student stood in darkness. It mattered not how much Nicodemus knew or what honors he had received. This man needed to be reborn. So positive was Jesus about this that He said, "Except a man be born of water and of the Spirit, he cannot enter into the kingdom of God." John 3:5.

There is no alternative: He that is born but once dies twice—the death all men face (Hebrews 9:27) and the eternal death following the judgment (Revelation 21:8). But he that is born twice dies but once, for after the resurrection he will live throughout eternity. Without the Holy Spirit there can be no rebirth, and without the rebirth there can be no spiritual life. All who will be sons and daughters of God therefore must be born by the Spirit. Why is this? Why must man be born again?

At creation the Father and the Son worked together. When Christ spoke, the Holy Spirit immediately carried His commands into effect. The Holy Spirit cooperated so that the thing which the Word called into existence existed instantly. In the second verse of the Bible Moses introduced the Spirit as moving upon the face of the waters. (Genesis 1:2.)

In all the creative activities of God which followed, the Holy Spirit played a vital role. Job said, "By his spirit he [God] hath garnished the heavens." Job 26:13. And in Psalm 104:30 we read, "Thou sendest forth thy spirit, they are created." At creation the Holy Spirit, symbolized as the breath of God, infused life into the clay. Job 33:4 says, "The spirit of God hath made me, and the breath of the Almighty hath given me life."

But man disobeyed God and partook of the forbidden fruit, thus causing the Spirit that had given him both spiritual and physical life to leave him. Adam then experienced spiritual death, though his physical existence persisted. He began to realize something of the awfulness of the sin he had committed. His nature had now become corrupt and vile; sin had poisoned his whole being. Man had become a slave—he had forfeited his power to choose. The Holy Spirit, the source of a righteous life, had withdrawn. Adam felt a gnawing emptiness, a frightening aloneness; he shivered in a nakedness of soul, fearfully looking for judgment, a terror akin to that which the finally impenitent must suffer.

Then God stepped in to offer man a second chance. God again gave him the power of choice—He made it possible for him to receive the Spirit back into his life. In the gospel promise of Genesis 3:15 God promised hope for fallen man. Man could turn to God or stay on Satan's ground. But he must choose. All who turn from the world to God and

11

accept the Holy Spirit, allowing Him to beget a new life within, are "born again." God accomplishes this creative process by the same Holy Spirit that begot Jesus. The invisible working of the Holy Spirit resembles the wind that cannot be seen, but the evidences of the Spirit's presence within will be seen in the daily life of all who are born again. (John 3:7.)

Regeneration or re-creation may be likened to the process of metamorphosis, or transformation, by which a caterpillar becomes a butterfly. Putting wings on a worm does not make it a butterfly. A worm's very nature has to be changed before it can become a butterfly. In conversion the Holy Spirit infuses new life energies into our souls. New purposes thrill through our being, new attitudes develop, new motives prompt our actions, the virtues and graces exemplified in the life of Jesus begin to be revealed in our lives. The same Holy Spirit that assisted in the creation of man brings about his re-creation. "God our Saviour [that is, the Lord Jesus Christ] . . . saved us, by the washing of regeneration, and renewing of the Holy Ghost." Titus 3:4, 5.

In Eden God generated man, that is, He brought him into being, gave him existence. By sin man became degenerated; his life processes reversed, and instead of being a "living" soul he became a "dying" soul. But now through the merits of Christ's sacrifice on Calvary and the gift of the Holy Spirit man may be regenerated, made anew, having the holy motives, the noble desires, the grand aims that God originally purposed he should have.

Christ's nativity is a pledge that whosoever will may experience a rebirth and become a son of God. Unless a man be born again by the Spirit, he is only a dying man, without hope, wandering about in the wilderness of a doomed world. He who fails to be born of the Spirit locks the gates of glory against his own soul. Those who are born again and stay faithful know the freedom of sins forgiven and live in joyful anticipation of the great day when Jesus shall come in flaming glory to gather His own.

Receiving the Spirit—
"By the Hearing of Faith"

You are important, for Christ died for you. God thinks it just as important that you be saved as that Peter, Paul, or John be saved. All the provisions of Calvary, including the gift of the Holy Spirit, are for you—as though you were the only one to benefit by them. They are yours upon one condition: acceptance by faith.

Some say, "But I have no faith." That isn't true. The Bible says, "God hath dealt to every man the measure of faith." Romans 12:3. God offers this gift to all. We are to receive and cherish it. We should pray as the disciples prayed, "Increase our faith." Luke 17:5. A distressed father brought his demon-possessed son to Jesus for healing and in his great extremity cried out, "Lord, I believe; help thou mine unbelief." Mark 9:24. Jesus heard his prayer; so will He hear ours. The "spirit of faith" (2 Corinthians 4:13) will provide all the faith we need. How? By the Word: "Faith cometh by hearing, and hearing by the word of God." Romans 10:17.

Nicodemus heard the Master say, "Except a man be born of water and of the Spirit, he cannot enter into the kingdom of God." John 3:5. And 1 Peter 1:23 says, "Being born again, not of corruptible seed, but of incorruptible, by the word of God, which liveth and abideth for ever." One text says we are born of the Spirit, and another that we are born by the Word. Can these two texts be reconciled? Yes!

Every seed has in it the germ of life. Take the germ of life out of a seed, and the seed becomes worthless. The germ of life in the Word is the Holy Spirit. By this agency God begets a new life in the hearts of believers. When the Bible reader receives the Word of God, the "incorruptible" "seed," he also receives the Holy Spirit, for the Holy Spirit accompanies the Word as it is read by those who are honest in heart. But what does it mean to "receive" the Word of God and consequently the Holy Spirit?

John 1:12 says, "As many as received him, to them gave he power to become the sons of God, even to them that believe on his name." John made believing the equivalent of receiving. Hearers become believers, and believers are receivers.

How do we receive the Holy Spirit? Paul asked

this question twice in Galatians 3:2-5: "Received ye the Spirit by the works of the law, or by the hearing of faith? . . . He therefore that ministereth to you the Spirit, . . . doeth he it by the works of the law, or by the hearing of faith?" Paul indicated the answer by his questions. We receive the Spirit not because of anything we do but "by the hearing of faith." To believe is to receive.

The Holy Spirit is Christ's gift to His spiritual children. It cannot be earned. Not by study, nor by sacrifice, nor by any sort of works that man may devise may we earn this gift. Simon Magus received such a rebuke by Peter as to forever close the door to the thought that the Holy Spirit might be obtained in any other way than by faith. Peter said, "Thy money perish with thee, because thou hast thought that the gift of God may be purchased with money." Acts 8:20. The Holy Spirit is spoken of here as "the gift of God." A gift is not earned; it is received.

To receive the Holy Spirit we need only believe in God's promises and through faith appropriate them to our lives. "Christ hath redeemed us from the curse of the law . . . that we might receive the promise of the Spirit through faith." Galatians 3:13, 14. Notice the words "receive . . . through faith." Faith in what? Faith in God's promise. According to 2 Corinthians 1:20-22, "all the promises of God in him are yea, and in him Amen. . . . Now he which . . . hath anointed us, is God; who hath also . . . given the earnest of the Spirit in our hearts." The faith we

16

exhibit in accepting Christ and in receiving the Spirit is faith supplied to us by God. (Ephesians 2: 8.) The Holy Spirit is a gift, and the faith by which we receive it is a gift. We are to believe in that gift and accept it. And that is how we may be born again, born of the Spirit.

Christians–
Those Anointed
by the Spirit

Are you a Christian? If you have any doubts about it, if you are not quite sure, your testimony for Christ is worthless. The blind man to whom Christ gave sight had no doubts about it. The dead that He raised again to life knew they were alive. You cannot be a Christian and not know it.

If you have unconfessed, unforgiven, and unforsaken sins in your life, whatever your profession, you are not a Christian. The Christian has the inner witness of the Spirit that he is a child of God. Paul said, "The Spirit itself beareth witness with our spirit, that we are the children of God." Romans 8:16. Right now we may know we are God's children, born from above.

He who thinks himself a Christian because of his church membership, his honesty in business dealings, his standing as a good citizen and a good neighbor, misunderstands the meaning of the word *Christian.*

When the church at Jerusalem sent Barnabas to Antioch to care for the developing interest there, what kind of man did they send? The Book of Acts says, "He was a good man, and full of the Holy Ghost." And what resulted from the work of this leader inspired by the Holy Spirit? Luke stated, "Much people was added unto the Lord." "And the disciples were called Christians first in Antioch." Acts 11:24, 26. Evidently these disciples had so much in them of what Christ had had in Him that the people decided the only appropriate name for them was "Christian." What a tribute!

If you have in you what Jesus had, you are a Christian. The disciples of Antioch had in them the same Holy Spirit who had given Jesus power.

"We have found the Messias," Andrew exclaimed. (John 1:41.) Ever since Adam and Eve had been driven from Eden, the world had lived in anticipation of the coming of the Messiah. The word *Messiah* is a Hebrew word. The Greek form of the word is "Christ," and the English equivalent is "The Anointed." Andrew was saying that God's Anointed had come, and that he had found Him. What an announcement!

Two thousand years ago the name Jesus was common in Israel. But there has been only one Jesus

19

to whom God gave the title "Christ." John the Baptist, who viewed the anointing of Jesus, declared, "I saw the Spirit descending from heaven like a dove, and it abode upon him." John 1:32. At that time the Father said, "Thou art my beloved Son; in thee I am well pleased." Luke 3:22.

When the Apostle Peter later presented the gospel to Cornelius, a Gentile and a Roman centurion, he emphasized one grand central truth: "God anointed Jesus of Nazareth with the Holy Ghost." Acts 10:38. God Himself did the anointing. God used no intermediate agency, no prophet, priest, or preacher.

Following His anointing Jesus spent forty days in the wilderness tempted by the devil. After this ordeal "Jesus returned in the power of the Spirit" (Luke 4:14) and went to Nazareth, where He gave the Sabbath discourse. Taking the Sacred Scroll, He read from a prophecy of Isaiah, who centuries before had foretold His anointing: "The Spirit of the Lord God is upon me; because the Lord hath anointed me." Isaiah 61:1. Then He applied this prophecy to Himself, saying, "This day is this scripture fulfilled in your ears." (Luke 4:18, 21.)

The fact that Jesus, one of their fellow townsmen, claimed the Messiahship (the divine anointing) stirred up such a resentment in the hearts of the congregation that unless God had intervened, they would have murdered His Son that day. This issue still lives today. Many are willing to accept Jesus as a good man, a miracle worker, a great teacher, and even as a prophet, but like the Jews of Nazareth they revolt against accepting Him as the Anointed of God. This is the crux of the matter. To accept Jesus as the Anointed implies that we are willing to be anointed with the same Holy Spirit with which He was anointed. Basically, then, a Christian is one who not only believes that God anointed Jesus with the Holy Spirit, but also allows God to anoint him. The Apostle Paul states it, "He which . . . hath anointed us, is God." 2 Corinthians 1:21.

When converted, Paul "straightway . . . preached Christ," "proving that this is very Christ." (Acts 9:20, 22.) The eloquent Apollos preached Christ: "He mightily convinced the Jews, . . . shewing by the scriptures that Jesus was Christ." Acts 18:28. The two words *Jesus Christ,* coupled together so often throughout the New Testament, underscore the fact that Jesus was the Anointed of God.

No one preached a funeral sermon for Jesus. But Peter, God's mouthpiece at Pentecost, preached a glorious resurrection sermon. He quoted the prophecies that foretold the resurrection of Jesus, the Anointed, and concluded, "Therefore let all the house of Israel know assuredly, that God hath made that same Jesus, whom ye have crucified, both Lord and Christ." Acts 2:36.

The Spirit moved the listening throng, who now realized that Jesus was indeed the Christ, to cry out, "Men and brethren, what shall we do?"

21

Peter replied, "Repent, and be baptized every one of you in the name of Jesus Christ." Then Peter went on to promise every one who thus accepted Jesus as the Anointed of God the same anointing that Jesus had had: "Ye shall receive the gift of the Holy Ghost." Acts 2:38.

Brought before King Agrippa, Paul preached Christ so fervently that the king cried out, "Almost thou persuadest me to be a Christian." Acts 26:28. But the king never humbled himself to accept Jesus as the Christ and receive the anointing of the Spirit. Many feel that they are Christians, yet they have never received the anointing of the Spirit. But all who have been anointed with the Spirit will enjoy both the fellowship of the Spirit and fellowship in the Spirit with their fellow Christians.

The Heavenly Guest

Unless you are a spiritual orphan, the Holy Ghost has taken up a permanent abode in your heart. On the night preceding His crucifixion Jesus told His disciples that He would send them "another Comforter." In the original Greek one of His promises in regard to this Comforter reads: "I will not leave you orphans, I will come to you." John 14:18. He wanted His disciples to know that the Comforter would replace His personal presence. Even though He knew they would be slow to comprehend, Jesus told them that God would give to them His Spirit, the very same Spirit that had accompanied Him throughout His earthly sojourn. As "another" Comforter, the Holy Spirit would stand in Christ's stead and provide for them the same inner assurance that Christ's personal presence had provided.

Strange, eventful happenings faced the disciples, the meaning of which they would not immediately understand. They would see the earth mantled with darkness, feel the solid ground quake beneath their feet, and hear Christ's last piercing cry from the cross. They were to carry His lifeless form to Joseph's new tomb. And then they were to experience a painful loneliness—they would feel like orphans. But Jesus did not intend that they should be orphans. At His very first meeting with them after His resurrection, "he breathed on them," saying, "Receive ye the Holy Ghost." John 20:22.

In Old English the word *ghost* had a more personal connotation than the word *spirit*. In effect, Jesus invited His disciples to receive a person. No one who knows the indwelling presence of this divine Guest will ever feel alone. The action of receiving is vital, however. The heavenly Guest offers companionship only to those who invite Him into their lives.

Jesus admonishes today, "Receive ye the Holy Guest." God has never forced any to be a spiritual orphan, an outcast, or a derelict. He never abandons any man. Rather, man forsakes God. "Your iniquities have separated between you and your God." Isaiah 59:2. Through disobedience man has made himself a stranger, an alien—a spiritual vagabond.

God longs to dwell with every one of His children. That, indeed, is the meaning of Christ's Incarnation and the ultimate purpose of the cross. But in the natural man—that is, the unconverted person— the place that God has made for Himself to occupy is filled with an impostor. Nevertheless, God is not deterred in His desire to dwell in man because of an impostor's presence. He freely offers liberation to all who will choose Christ. If man desires, Jesus will evict the deceiver and send the Holy Spirit to indwell the soul.

To believe in Christ is to receive the Holy Guest into our hearts. This is to be a permanent relationship. To underscore this Jesus told of a certain man whose house or soul had been swept and garnished, his sins forgiven, and the evil spirit driven out. But this man, like many others, failed to continue welcoming the Holy Spirit into his heart. Later the evil spirit returned, and, finding the house empty, he recruited seven other evil spirits, and the eight of them invaded the old premises to set up a new tyranny far worse than the first. (Matthew 12:43-45.) The soul will not remain unoccupied. It will be indwelt by either unholy spirits or by the heavenly Guest.

The tragic story of Saul, Israel's first king, illustrates how a man may lose God's Spirit. God gave young Saul His Spirit. (1 Samuel 10:6.) Saul gladly obeyed at first. But later, when reproved for disobedience, Saul became moody, dissident, and disagreeable. He wanted to be a part-time believer, a part-way follower. Affable one moment, he would indulge a violent temper tantrum the next. Thus he developed a split personality. But God never works in partnership with Satan. Christ said, "Ye cannot serve God and mammon." Matthew 6:24. The heavenly Guest left Saul, and an evil spirit possessed him. (1 Samuel 16:14.) Eventually life itself became so intolerable to Saul that he committed suicide.

Saul's successor, King David, also faltered in obedience and became a prodigal son in Heaven's sight. Sin made David's devotions meaningless. He sang the songs of Zion, bowed his head in worship, went through the other motions of religion, but existed as only a wooden man, an actor, not a worshiper. The heavenly Guest could not continue to dwell within while he refused to confess the sin in his heart.

Months went by. Then God sent Nathan the prophet to expose to David the guilt that plagued his soul. With the dreadful history of Saul before him, he saw that the Holy Spirit soon would give up striving with him and leave him forever to that merciless spirit that had plagued his predecessor. In desperation David prayed, "Create in me a clean heart, O God." He realized that heart cleansing preceded Spirit indwelling.

David's prayer continued: "Renew a right spirit within me." Psalm 51:10. Realizing that without the Holy Spirit he would be a spiritual castaway and banished forever from God's presence, David implored, "Take not thy holy spirit from me."

As assurance of forgiveness came, David pledged

26

himself to become a missionary witness: "Restore unto me the joy of thy salvation; and uphold me with thy free spirit, then will I teach transgressors thy ways; and sinners shall be converted unto thee." Psalm 51:10-13.

Today we have the same merciful God, and we need the indwelling of the heavenly Guest just as urgently as did David. There may be no active hostility toward the heavenly Guest in our soul, but there may not be any genuine hospitality offered Him either. Satan overcomes many by little sins, mere trivia. They love the things of this life, its pleasures, its sweet nothings. For many, life's little goings and comings crowd out the fellowship of the Spirit just as effectively as would some great sin.

We must recognize that activity, busyness—even in the Lord's work—cannot substitute for the presence of the Holy Guest.

The Fellowship
of the Spirit

"If any man have not the Spirit of Christ, he is none of his." Romans 8:9. The Bible nowhere qualifies this arresting statement. It offers no alternatives, no exceptions. The presence of the Spirit of Christ in the heart is the test of discipleship. Without Christ's Spirit the soul is empty, void, and waste. If we know Jesus as our Saviour, we shall have the presence of His Spirit. The presence of the Holy Spirit in our hearts is to be a joyful assurance that we belong to Him. The sequence is, "After that ye believed, ye were sealed with that holy Spirit of promise." Ephesians 1:13.

The Bible offers no substitute for the "fellowship of the Spirit." (Philippians 2:1.) Fellowship involves more than a "touch-and-go" relationship. There should never be a time day or night when we act or think without an awareness of the Spirit's presence. And when we heed the promptings of the Holy Spirit, this awareness awakens new and holy motivations.

The unity between the Father, Son, and Holy Spirit may be illustrated by a candle: The wax represents the Father, the Source of all blessings; the wick represents the Son, the One through whom and by whom all heavenly blessings are brought to us; the fire on the candle represents the Holy Spirit, who flashes the light of truth into the soul.

The light of truth shining within our hearts provides evidence of the presence of the Holy Three. (1 John 1:3.) As the Father sent the Son into the world that every man might become acquainted with the Godhead, so together they have sent the Holy Spirit into the hearts of all who believe that every disciple might have light and enjoy spiritual fellowship with all members of the Godhead. (Galatians 4:4-6.)

God wants to come into our lives by His Spirit. He will meet us just where we are. The Holy Spirit wants us to have the fellowship blessings of mutual understanding, warmth of affection, and communion. Every response to the Spirit makes this blessed fellowship more real. On the other hand, the irresponsive soul grows cold to the promptings of the Spirit. To resist light is to resist the fellowship of the Spirit, and such a course can only eventuate in a frigid and painful aloneness.

Many look back to when the Spirit led them to accept Jesus. But they remain strangely silent about their daily walk with Jesus. They lack that "something more" which the abiding presence of the Spirit will furnish. Doctrines, theories, and activities are not enough. To become apostles of Christ, the disciples themselves needed something more—the fellowship of the Spirit. (Acts 1; 2.)

Learning that the Samaritans, under the ministry of Philip, had accepted Jesus as the Christ, the church at Jerusalem sent Peter and John to minister to the new converts that "something more"—the Holy Spirit. (Acts 8.) Cornelius and his household also needed something more. They were living up to all the light they had. But they needed more. Not only did they need to know of Jesus, but they needed to receive the infilling of His Spirit. (Acts 10.) And when Paul found disciples at Ephesus who had not even heard of the Holy Spirit, he immediately instructed them so that they might receive the Spirit. (Acts 19.)

All who simply know of Jesus stand in need of something more—the presence in their life of a Person, a divine Person, the Holy Spirit. The daily infilling of the Spirit keeps the experience fresh, new, and growing.

How the Spirit Handles
That "Guilt Complex"

What happens to the sins of one who accepts Christ and receives His Spirit?

A woman's voice—piercing, urgent—rang through the halls of a hospital where I once worked. "What am I going to do with all my sins?" she cried out as the orderlies wheeled her toward the operating room. Quickly the nurses gathered about, trying in vain to quiet her. The operating-room door opened, and her last word, shrill and distinct, just as the door closed, was "sins." As a newly baptized Christian, my heart went out in sympathy to that suffering, sin-sick soul! How I have hoped that someone pointed her to Jesus, "the Lamb of God, which taketh away the sin of the world." (John 1:29.)

Where shall we go with our sins? We can't leave them at home or at some depot. We can't leave them in the doctor's office or on the psychiatrist's couch. We can't give them away to any man, be he preacher or priest. Only Jesus can take away our sins.

Calamities, disasters, and destructions have plagued our planet throughout the centuries, but nothing so terribly grinds down, wears out, and oppresses the soul as sin. Disease may wrack the body and waste the frame, but no physical torture can compare to the inner anguish caused by guilt. Guilt gnaws incessantly and relentlessly at the heart. Like a hideous specter lurking in the dark shadows of the soul, guilt haunts us, mocks our pleasures, and sneers at our successes. Guilt produces a diabolical brood of evil fruits—irritability, bitterness, sarcasm, criticism, disaffection, restlessness, suspicion, and hate. Many a person has become mentally ill while vainly trying to excuse, palliate, and justify his wrongdoings.

Like a red flare in the night, guilt warns that unforgiven sin exists in the soul. We cannot be rid of guilt without first getting rid of sin. And since there is no way to change a deed that has already been done, the plight of human beings seems hopeless. But there is hope for those who will accept the forgiveness that Jesus so generously offers.

Christ can provide forgiveness because He never sinned. Christ, the Sinless One, bore our sins, and became sin for us. He did it for everybody, but only those who believe in Him can be benefited. Only

those who by repentance and confession give up and
give over their sins to Him and accept His righteousness in exchange for their sins can receive the gift He
has to offer. (2 Corinthians 5:21.) As the Holy Spirit
flashes this vital truth into the soul of the sinner, it
awakens faith, and the grateful heart responds to the
love that made such a provision possible. Indeed,
"we love him, because he first loved us." (1 John 4:
19.) Those who truly love Jesus are eager to sur-
render their sins to Him and to forsake the paths of
sin. Christians will love Christ too much to carelessly
wound His heart afresh. The "guilt complex," as it is
so frequently spoken of today, is truly complex, but
its remedy is quite simple.

The accusings of conscience, the unhappy restlessness, the deep dissatisfactions, the bitter resent-
ments that build up within the soul, largely result
because divine approval has been withdrawn. The
Holy Spirit, the divine Comforter who encourages
man when he does right and assures him that in doing
right he is fulfilling the grand purposes of his
existence, withdraws that approval when man does
wrong. He can't comfort the sinner in his sins. Without the fellowship of the Spirit the sinner has no
peace with himself or with anyone else. Isaiah said,
"There is no peace, saith my God, to the wicked."
Isaiah 57:21.

God sends His Holy Spirit to the sinner to bring
about reconciliation and restore the broken fellowship. The Spirit works by helping the sinner see how

God looks at sin—to see that sin cost the life of Jesus. The Holy Spirit leads the sinner to see the true nature of sin: that sin is intrinsically evil, diabolical, wicked, frightening, and totally reprehensible; that the sting of death is in every sin. He helps the wrongdoer to understand that God cannot ignore sin or brush it aside; that in order to save man from sin and its consequences, Jesus Himself had to feel as the sinner feels when plagued with guilt, and upon the cross suffer as the unrepentant will have to suffer in the final destruction of the wicked. Stated in another way, the Spirit actually *exposes* sin in its naked ugliness to the sinner; and when the sinner sees its exceeding sinfulness and realizes that only the death of the sinless Son of God could possibly atone for his sin, he becomes disturbed. This is called *conviction*. Conviction is intended to lead to repentance. Conviction gives evidence that the Holy Spirit is working in the heart.

Though the Holy Spirit brings conviction, He does not stop there, for His purpose is to restore fellowship with God, to banish fear, apprehension, and alarm. The evil spirit suggests, "Better not take your stand for Jesus now," or "Don't take your stand until you know you will stick by it," or "Religion will make a fool out of you." But God does not prompt these thoughts. The spirit of fear is not from God. (2 Timothy 1:7.)

The steps that the sinner takes to receive reconciliation and freedom from guilt are simple. All who repent of their sins, confess them, and believe that for Christ's sake they are forgiven, will know that their guilt has been lifted. The pardoned soul rests upon God's promises. "Therefore being justified by faith, we have peace with God through our Lord Jesus Christ." Romans 5:1. When the sinner has turned away from sin and forsaken it, the Comforter assures him that his sins are forgiven, and he rejoices in the fellowship of the Spirit.

If after a sinner has confessed Christ he should be un-Christlike in his behavior or falter in his obedience in a moment of weakness, he should not give up but should go immediately to Jesus and with repentance and confession claim anew Christ's sacrifice on Calvary. Though the Christian stumbles, God by no means casts him off. God will pardon the broken-hearted and repentant. This assurance is found in 1 John 2:1: "My little children, these things write I unto you, that ye sin not. And if any man sin, we have an advocate with the Father, Jesus Christ the righteous."

When David lost the presiding presence of the Holy Spirit in his life, guilt plagued his soul. He knew that happiness for him would never return without the Spirit. In penitence he prayed, "Renew a right spirit within me." Psalm 51:10. With the return of the Comforter David could exclaim, "O Lord, . . . my mouth shall shew forth thy praise." (Verse 15.)

The Personality
of the Spirit

"Another Comforter"! What could the Master mean? Could anyone take the Master's place? Could there ever be "another" who would be to the disciples all the Master had been? Yet in that upper-room meeting Jesus told them of Someone to follow Him who was to fill the place in their lives that He had filled, Someone empowered to act in His stead.

A patient became apprehensive when he learned that his doctor would be away for six months. "But you will be in good hands," the doctor said with assurance. "My brother and I went to medical college together, we have practiced together for twenty years, and we have often counseled together about your case. He knows as much about you as I do. You need not worry. My brother will be to you as my second self."

In sending this other Comforter Jesus in reality sent His "second self." Of this Comforter Jesus said, "He dwelleth with you, and shall be in you." John 14:17. The disciples had only dimly understood how Jesus as Emmanuel had been God *with* them, but now He spoke of "another" that was to dwell *in* them. This was too difficult for them to grasp as yet. Indeed, they would have to experience it in order to understand.

In these words Jesus prepared the way for His successor. He wanted His disciples to receive the Comforter as they would receive Him. And who was this Person of whom He spoke? None other than the Third Person of the Godhead! Only another member of the Godhead could ever be to them all that He had been to them.

Many have been deceived into equating the Spirit of God with an abstraction. They speak of the Holy Spirit as merely an influence. But while the Spirit has influence, He is much more than an influence—He is a Person, a divine Person. To be sure, the Holy Spirit has power, "the power of the Highest" (Luke 1:35), yet the Spirit is not power in any abstract sense like gravity or electricity.

In announcing His personal representative and successor, Jesus did not mean to withdraw His affections from His disciples. Jesus would be closer to them by His Spirit than if He had remained with them limited by the flesh. The love of God would still be shed abroad in their hearts. Indeed, the Spirit would be to them as Christ's personal presence. Having His Spirit *within* them, His disciples would feel as He felt, see things as He saw them, love sinners as He loved them, and become more like Him than would have been possible if Jesus had remained with them. Indwelt by the Spirit of Christ, they would be privileged to know the real Christ. They would have *in* them the same Spirit that had indwelt their Master. Thus they would know the "inside" Christ because the inside Christ can be known only as the Holy Spirit reveals Him. (1 Corinthians 12:3.)

The baptismal formula given by Jesus makes plain the deity of the Holy Spirit. "Go ye therefore, and teach all nations, baptizing them in the name of the Father, and of the Son, and of the Holy Ghost." Matthew 28:19. The apostolic benediction states this truth somewhat differently: "The grace of the Lord Jesus Christ, and the love of God, and the communion of the Holy Ghost, be with you all. Amen." 2 Corinthians 13:14.

The Three Persons of the Godhead are one in essence, one in purpose, and one in motive. The interrelationships of the Holy Three can never be grasped by finite minds. But we do know of Jesus, and He has said, "He that hath seen me hath seen the Father." John 14:9. So to the extent that we are acquainted with the Son we are also acquainted with the Father. And to the same extent we will be ac-

38

quainted with the Holy Spirit.

The members of the Godhead resemble a chain of three links. The two outer links represent the Father and the Son. The center link, the one that binds the two outer links together, represents the Holy Spirit. In one Scripture reference Paul called the Third Person of the Godhead "the Spirit of Christ" *and* "the Spirit of God." (Romans 8:9.) In other words, the Spirit belongs to the Son as much as He does to the Father. He is the middle link.

The Holy Spirit as a divine Person exercises all the prerogatives of Deity. He had an important part in man's creation, and His role in the work of re-creation or regeneration is just as prominent. (Titus 3:5.) He is present everywhere (Psalm 139:7-10) and is not subject to death, for He is called the "eternal Spirit" (Hebrews 9:14).

Since the Holy Spirit distributes spiritual gifts "to every man severally as he will" (1 Corinthians 12:11), He must possess personality, for the "will" is an essential attribute of personality. The Scriptures speak of "the mind of the Spirit." (Romans 8:27.) And they declare that He knows what God knows: "The things of God knoweth . . . the Spirit of God." 1 Corinthians 2:11.

Moreover, Bible writers describe the Spirit as a teacher (1 Corinthians 2:13), a witness (Romans 8:16), an intercessor (Romans 8:26), a guide (John 16:13), an administrator (Acts 20:28), and one with whom we are to enjoy fellowship (Philippians

2:1). These functions indicate personality.

Emotions also are associated with personality. An impersonal influence cannot impart love. But "the love of God is shed abroad [implanted] in our hearts by the Holy Ghost." (Romans 5:5.) Can anyone carry on a conversation with vapor or mist? Can he lie to the darkness? These do not have personality. But Ananias and Sapphira died because they lied to the Holy Spirit. They had "not lied unto men, but unto God." (Acts 5:3, 4.)

In those precious last moments that He had with His disciples, Jesus explained as much as His followers could possibly understand about the One who was to take His place. In spite of the fact that the word *spirit* in the Greek is neuter and takes the pronoun "it," Christ used the masculine pronoun "He" or "Him" twenty-four times when referring to the Holy Spirit during this talk with them. (John 14–16.) The Master wanted His disciples to see the Spirit not as something mystic, ethereal, or nebulous, but as a real person. Those today who understand this will not be led by impressions, phobias, quirks, hunches, imaginings, and such. Impressions may be, and very often are, of our fallen nature. Satan can give impressions. But the honest-hearted will know the leadings of the Holy Spirit because He never leads anyone contrary to a "Thus saith the Lord."

40

Symbols of
the Holy Spirit

The Scriptures use several symbols to represent the offices, functions, and ministrations of the Third Person of the Godhead. These emblems, figures, and representations help to portray the magnitude of the Spirit's power and work.

Oil: The oil used in connection with the ancient sanctuary symbolized the Spirit's presence. God commanded that anointing oil be used at the dedication of the Tabernacle to signify its setting apart for holy purposes. In Israel's economy, prophets, priests, and kings were anointed for holy office. God thus indicated that the Holy Spirit would guide these men in discharging their duties.

For example, God instructed Elijah to anoint his

successor, Elisha. (1 Kings 19:16.) Samuel anointed David in the midst of his brethren, and "the Spirit of the Lord came upon David from that day forward." (1 Samuel 16:13.) At Aaron's dedication to the priesthood joy prevailed. David commented, "Behold, how good and how pleasant it is for brethren to dwell together in unity! It is like the precious ointment upon the head, . . . even Aaron's." Psalm 133:1, 2.

Similarly, the gospel provides an unction or an anointing of the Spirit for every believer. The Spirit sets apart every born-again soul to live a dedicated life. (1 John 2:20, 27.)

Water: People living in the Near East call water the gift of God. As there can be no life without water, so there can be no spiritual life without the Holy Spirit. Paul not only associated the Spirit with life (Romans 8:2), but he even declared, "the Spirit is life" (Romans 8:10). Isaiah equated water with the Spirit: "I will pour water upon him that is thirsty, and floods upon the dry ground: I will pour out my spirit upon thy seed." Isaiah 44:3. Of Jesus' statement about "rivers of living water" that were to flow from each believer, John commented, "But this spake he of the Spirit, which they that believe on him should receive." (John 7:38, 39.) In vision John saw "a pure river of water of life . . . proceeding out of the throne of God." (Revelation 22:1.) Over half a millennium earlier Ezekiel had seen in vision waters issuing out of the restored sanctuary. (Ezekiel 47:

1-7.) Both prophets picture the blessing as coming from the throne of God.

When Israel asked for water, God told Moses to strike a rock. When he did so, water flowed freely from the rock. (Exodus 17:1-7.) Paul later explained, "They drank of that spiritual Rock that followed them: and that Rock was Christ." 1 Corinthians 10:4. Christ sustained and led Israel. At the cross He bore the stroke that He might provide the sustaining Spirit for all who thirst.

Bible writers associated water with regeneration (Titus 3:5) and the new birth (John 3:5). Thus in a special sense, baptism, immersion in water, symbolizes spiritual cleansing. (Acts 22:16.)

Allusions in the Bible to springs, fountains, wells, rivers, dew, showers, and rain in many cases refer to the ministry of the Spirit. Not only are the faithful to drink out of the wells of salvation (Isaiah 12:3), but they are to dispense living waters to others; that is, they are to let the Spirit in them flow out as rivers of blessings for others (John 4:14; 7:38).

Wind: The mighty rushing wind at Pentecost announced the presence of the Third Person of the Godhead. (Acts 2:1-4.) The wind also portrays the new birth. "The wind bloweth where it listeth, and thou hearest the sound thereof, but canst not tell whence it cometh, and whither it goeth: so is every one that is born of the Spirit." John 3:8. The Spirit, like the wind, works invisibly—only its effects are seen.

Fire: Fire consumes the dross and refines the

gold. When an angel touched Isaiah's lips with a "live coal . . . from off the altar," the Lord said to him, "Thine iniquity is taken away." (Isaiah 6:6, 7.)

Fire denotes spiritual energy, divine fervor, penetrating enthusiasm, holy inspiration. The passive soul touched by the fire of the Spirit becomes possessed with a burning passion to save souls. Neither education, training, nor environment brings about this change. The Holy Spirit creates it.

John the Baptist, whom Jesus described as a burning and shining light (John 5:35), prophesied of the Messiah, "He shall baptize you with the Holy Ghost and with fire." Luke 3:16. After Christ's return to heaven He did baptize His followers with the Holy Spirit. On the day of Pentecost cloven tongues of fire sat upon 120 disciples of Christ, and they went forth as blazing torches and set ablaze 3,000 other tapers that very day. (Acts 2:1-4, 41.)

When persecution later broke out in Jerusalem, the disciples "went every where preaching the word." (Acts 8:4.) Thus fires were lighted here and there and continued to spread until within thirty years salvation's thrilling story had encompassed the Roman world. (Romans 1:8.) Bible prophecy depicts in time's last hour yet another gospel conflagration when the message of Christ's return will be heralded with power "to every nation, and kindred, and tongue, and people." (Revelation 14:6.)

God needs more such flames of fire today. How can one become a firebrand for Christ? By fully

44

accepting Christ and His Spirit as did the totally committed Paul, who said, "I am made all things to all men, that I might by all means save some." 1 Corinthians 9:22.

Total commitment led Martin Luther to testify before the Diet of Worms, "Unless therefore I am convinced by the testimony of Scripture, . . . *I cannot and I will not retract.* . . . Here I stand, I can do no other; may God help me. Amen."

Total commitment led John Knox to pray, "Give me Scotland or I die."

Total commitment led John Wesley to exclaim, "I look upon the world as my parish."

Total commitment led William Carey to reply, "Serving Christ is my business, I cobble shoes for a living."

Total commitment led David Livingstone to insist, "I will place no value on anything I have or may possess except in relation to the Kingdom of Christ."

Ministers ablaze for Christ and "fervent in spirit" will cross the hottest deserts, scale the steepest mountains, defy the densest jungles, pierce iron and bamboo curtains, penetrate Muslim and Hindu strongholds, invade the most forbidding cities, to conquer the unconquerable. They will scorn the unheroic, the mediocre, and unchallenging, to spend and be spent, do and dare, give and go, in utter abandon following the Spirit's direction for the salvation of souls and the glory of God.

The Spirit
Convicts of Sin

In a telegraphic description made by Christ just before His death He pointed out three aspects of the Spirit's work. "He will convince the world of sin and of righteousness and of judgment." John 16:8, R.S.V. In explaining the first of these, Jesus said, "Of sin, because they believe not on me." Verse 9.

The Bible mentions four general categories of sin. First is the sin of commission: "Sin is the transgression of the law." 1 John 3:4. Second, the sin of omission: "To him that knoweth to do good, and doeth it not, to him it is sin." James 4:17. Third, the sin of coming short of glorifying God in our acts: "All have sinned, and come short of the glory of

THE SPIRIT CONVICTS OF SIN

God." Romans 3:23. Fourth, the sin of unbelief: "Whatsoever is not of faith is sin." Romans 14:23.

Of all sins, the sin of unbelief looms most treacherous because it destroys the means whereby we receive forgiveness. Unbelief is subtle, deceiving, and often unperceived. Beginning with the voicing of a doubt as an opinion, it soon becomes an attitude of the mind. Like a chancre within the heart, it slowly eats away. Finally, it bewitches its victim, fouls the character, and damns the soul. "He that doubteth is damned." Romans 14:23. If you are inclined to doubt, you should listen to Christ's words spoken to Thomas, the disciple who had this weakness: "Be not faithless, but believing." John 20:27. Pray as did the father of the demoniac lad: "Lord, I believe; help thou mine unbelief." Mark 8:24.

We must have faith to please God. "Without faith it is impossible to please him." Hebrews 11:6. Of all the doctrines set forth in the Bible faith receives by far the most attention.

The "spirit of faith" works to stimulate faith and to create within the soul a desire for greater faith. (2 Corinthians 4:13.) The great goal, of course, is that we may experience righteousness by faith: "We through the Spirit wait for the hope of righteousness by faith." Galatians 5:5.

The word *convince* in John 16:8, R.S.V., can be used in a judicial context: that is, to arrest, apprehend, convict, and bring under surveillance. The Holy Spirit acts as a sheriff apprehending a lawbreaker and saying, "You are under arrest." In effect, the Holy Spirit brings the sinner to trial in the court of his own conscience and says, "You know you are guilty." The sinner experiences inner distress when he is made to acknowledge the verdict of his own conscience and sees himself a moral "convict," a fugitive from justice, an outlaw whose life is forfeited unless he can find pardon. We say he is under "conviction." Here is where many try to compromise with the Holy Spirit. Though the sinner knows that he has done wrong and feels restless, uneasy, and frustrated, yet his human nature squirms and twists trying to evade facing up to wrong. He often hides his guilt behind a disarming smile. Self, ever on the defensive, contests the verdict, and for obvious reasons, for self must die when sin is confessed and forsaken. Self fights for this present life. On the other hand, the Holy Spirit works to save the sinner from yielding to the fierce resistance or whimperings of self, for if self isn't slain, the soul must die.

The Holy Spirit does not remind the sinner of his sins that He might make him unhappy. He knows that sin is man's worst enemy; He has the sinner's present and eternal welfare in mind. But like a faithful doctor, He diagnoses the case and then presents Christ to the sinner as his only remedy.

When explaining the charter under which the Holy Spirit would operate, Jesus said that men would be convicted "of sin, because they believe not on me." (John 16:9.) The moment Adam sinned, he became a lost man. "By one man sin entered into the world." Romans 5:12. Every human being by heredity partakes of the weakened nature transmitted by Adam, but each is lost because of his own sins. Though all are lost, however, all may be redeemed upon one condition: belief in Christ's sacrifice on Calvary. Those who refuse to believe stand convicted by the Holy Spirit because they did not believe on Jesus.

The man who refuses to look in faith to Christ has "an evil heart of unbelief." (Hebrews 3:12.) Love has no greater argument to present to the sinner than the cross.

Those who believe in Christ are those who have realized their own sinfulness. The Holy Spirit has worked upon their hearts, convicting them of sin— but the work of the Spirit does not end here.

The Spirit Convicts
of Righteousness

The Spirit's work goes beyond convicting of sin. Jesus said that the Spirit would also convince the world of righteousness. The Spirit is able to do this, said Christ, "because I go to my Father, and ye see me no more." (John 16:10.) What is righteousness? Simply defined, it is right doing. Ezra declared of God, "Thou art righteous." Ezra 9:15. Said the psalmist, "The Lord is righteous in all his ways." Psalm 145:17. "In all his ways" includes His dealings with the bad as well as with the good, with devils as well as with the holy angels.

Since God is righteous, His law must be righteous. Indeed, "all thy commandments are righteousness." Psalm 119:172. No wonder the prophet Daniel exclaimed, "O Lord, righteousness belongeth unto thee." Daniel 9:7. And David insisted, "There is no unrighteousness in him." Psalm 92:15. There is nothing unrighteous in God's dealings with any of the creatures in His vast universe. His law and judgments, His love and mercy, His justice and pity, all manifest His righteousness. The term "righteousness" is somewhat like a basket; it holds all excellencies and all perfections. "Thy righteousness is an everlasting righteousness." Psalm 119:142.

But when we look at the unregenerate man, a different picture appears. Man is "filled with all unrighteousness." (Romans 1:29.) Of the billions upon billions of human beings that have trod the earth Paul declared, "There is none righteous, no, not one." Romans 3:10. Isaiah said, "All our righteousnesses are as filthy rags." Isaiah 64:6.

What is the possibility of reform? Can man make himself righteous? Is there any such thing as a spiritual self-improvement program? Can man ever completely reform himself? Self may be ever so disgusted with self—lament and mourn over its evil ways—but self will never overcome self; it can never cast itself out. Self may reform in some things, but whenever it works out some voluntary humility, it quickly brags about it. "See what 'I' have done," boasts self-attainment. God asks, "Can the Ethiopian change his skin, or the leopard his spots? then may ye also do good, that are accustomed to do evil." Jeremiah 13:23.

51

The office of the Holy Spirit is to make righteousness so attractive and so desirable to man that he will be willing to sacrifice his incorrigible self to obtain it. When the sinner sees the righteousness, the goodness, and the love of Christ, who willingly suffered as his substitute on the cross and died in his stead for his sins, gratitude wells up in his soul and he cries out, "I believe." When he accepts Christ, he receives forgiveness and with this Christ's righteousness. He stands justified before God through the merits of Christ's sinless life and shed blood.

Jesus was made sin for us "that we might be made the righteousness of God in him." (2 Corinthians 5: 21.) The Holy Spirit not only deals with the negative —sin—but with the positive—righteousness. When God forgives sin through faith in the merits of Christ's sacrifice, He imputes righteousness to the believer. The believer stands before God not only as though he had never sinned, but as though he had given God the same perfect obedience that Christ has given Him.

How can the Spirit convince man of righteousness? Jesus said, "Because I go to my Father." How can His going back to God convince us of this? Because God the Father would never have accepted Jesus back into heaven if there had been one stain of sin upon Him. Of Jesus we read, He "was in all points tempted like as we are, yet without sin." (Hebrews 4:15.) "Though he were a Son, yet learned he obedience by the things which he suffered." Hebrews 5:8.

He was "obedient unto death, even the death of the cross. Wherefore God also hath highly exalted him, and given him a name which is above every name." (Philippians 2:8, 9.) Because Jesus obeyed, God the Father accepted His righteousness.

How did Jesus develop His positive righteousness? Isaiah prophesied of Christ, "The spirit of the Lord shall rest upon him, . . . and shall make him of quick understanding in the fear of the Lord: . . . with righteousness shall he judge the poor. . . . And righteousness shall be the girdle of his loins." Isaiah 11:2-5. The Holy Spirit resting upon Christ enabled Him to live a righteous life. Because Christ Himself lived such a life, was Himself so filled with the Spirit, He could "go to the Father," or be resurrected; and because of this the Spirit could convict of righteousness. Only after Christ's life had demonstrated a perfect righteousness could the Spirit follow and Himself convict men that they should have the righteousness reflected in the life of Christ.

But the Spirit's work in convicting of righteousness encompassed more than convicting the sinner that Christ is righteous. It also includes convincing men that they may have this same righteousness. Justification has to do with that portion of a man's life which he has already lived—the sins committed in the past. (Romans 3:25.) But once justified does not mean always justified. The question naturally arises, How is the convert to live that unlived portion of his life that is yet future? Surely it is not to be lived

53

to the lusts of the flesh. (1 Peter 4:2.) To receive Christ involves accepting the righteousness that He lived out in His life 1,900 years ago and receiving the same Spirit that enabled Him to live the righteous life He lived then. It means that we should live "soberly, righteously, and godly, in this present world," just as Christ lived while on the earth. (Titus 2:12.) How can this be done? Through the indwelling of the Holy Spirit! "Walk in the Spirit, and ye shall not fulfil the lust of the flesh." Galatians 5:16. Thus the Holy Spirit goes a step further and uses the Christian to convince "the world . . . of righteousness"!

The Bible calls this growing up in Christ "sanctification." The sanctified believer behaves as Christ behaved. He has a progressive experience, continuing as long as life lasts. As justification is by faith (Romans 5:1), so sanctification is by faith (Acts 26:18). We receive justification by believing that Jesus took upon Himself the penalty for our guilt when He died for us. We experience sanctification as day by day we let the Holy Spirit do in us what He did in Jesus. Sanctification means obedience to the law through the Spirit. (Romans 15:16.) Sanctification may also be spoken of as imparted righteousness. "God hath . . . chosen you to salvation through sanctification of the Spirit." 2 Thessalonians 2:13.

The Spirit Convicts
of Judgment

Jesus also declared that the Spirit would convict the world "of judgment, because the prince of this world is judged." John 16:11.

Behind the play and counterplay of history, supernatural forces, good and evil, have waged an unceasing warfare. At the cross the great controversy between Christ and Satan became visible. Christ and Satan stood before an empaneled universe to be judged. One would be acquitted, the other condemned. The events that culminated in Christ's crucifixion would expose to the universe the inner feelings of each. Would Christ in the hour of test and trial accept some attitude of Satan and be brought under his dominion? When reviled, would He revile back? When outraged, would He strike back? When abused, insulted, tortured, and tormented, would Jesus become vindictive?

Behold the Lord of glory in shame. The Light of the world stands in the midst of darkness, but the darkness cannot put out the light of God's love. The Prince of life, seized with paroxysms of pain, chooses to die rather than be disloyal to God. The Sinless One is robed in sin, but His righteousness shines through. The universe stands amazed at the spectacle of the Creator in the hands of His creatures. Satan sits in the judgment seat ready to pronounce the death sentence. The world unseen sees it all: the rigged court, the false witnesses, the time-serving judge intimidated by the Jerusalem rabble.

Satan condemned the innocent One to the most cruel of deaths. A being lacking God's Spirit demonstrated what all who lack that Spirit when unrestrained would do. When unrestrained by the Spirit of God, the unconverted man inspired by him who "was a murderer from the beginning" (John 8:44) will act out all the evil that is in his carnal nature, even to perpetrating unprovoked murder.

Satan stood unmasked. Christ's death exonerated God and proved that He was in no way responsible for sin. John pulled the curtain back so that all might see what then took place in heaven. "And I heard a loud voice saying in heaven, Now is come salvation, and strength, and the kingdom of our God, and the power of his Christ: for the accuser of our brethren is cast down, which accused them before our God day and night." Revelation 12:10. Shortly before, Jesus had foretold Satan's eviction: "Now is the judgment of this world: now shall the prince of this world be cast out." John 12:31.

A court higher than any that Satan could convene witnessed the innocent One suffer death at the hands of Satan. God acted as Chief Justice, and every heavenly intelligence formed a part of the grand jury. This court, having examined Jesus under the searchlight of God's law, reversed the rigged verdicts of those courts which Satan had dominated. Heaven completely absolved our Lord and decreed that He should not be held in Satan's prison house of death. Death must not have dominion over Him whom Heaven judged innocent of any sin. Of the Hero of Calvary, Peter declared, "Whom God hath raised up, having loosed the pains of death: because it was not possible that he should be holden of it." Acts 2:24. And how was Christ raised from the dead? He was "quickened by the Spirit." (1 Peter 3:18.)

But though Satan stood unmasked and guilty at Calvary, man's judgment had not yet come. The awful fact remained that man had shared in this monstrous crime. We are all guilty, for we have all displayed the same evil traits toward one another and God that ran riot there.

Thank God, the accuser of the brethren is cast down. This would-be judge has been judged and but awaits the execution of his sentence. In Heaven's verdict all who follow Satan on earth can read their own doom. The Holy Spirit works to keep this before our minds, for as Satan was judged guilty of Christ's blood, so all his followers will ultimately be judged guilty as partakers with him in his reprehensible deed. And as Jesus stood exonerated before the universe, so all His followers will someday stand completely absolved, for their acceptance of Jesus will have shown that they desire to turn from the attributes of character that impelled Satan to perpetrate the diabolical outrage.

The Holy Spirit, then, not only convinces us that the prince of this world has been judged but that every member of the human family will also be judged. Man has two appointments, both of which he will inevitably meet: death and judgment. "It is appointed unto men once to die, but after this the judgment." Hebrews 9:27. "We must all appear before the judgment seat of Christ." 2 Corinthians 5: 10. And there will be nothing haphazard about this judgment—no favoritisms of any kind. God declares, "Judgment also will I lay to the line, and righteousness to the plummet." Isaiah 28:17.

The Spirit of God desires that every soul make preparation. All who respond to the Spirit's promptings will confess their sins and thus send them beforehand to judgment. "Some men's sins are open beforehand, going before to judgment; and some men they follow after." 1 Timothy 5:24.

Even now within the soul our conscience bears

witness either "accusing or else excusing" (Romans 2:15) our thoughts and the very intents of our hearts, our attitudes, and our conduct in order that we might be purged "by the spirit of judgment, and by the spirit of burning" (Isaiah 4:4).

As the Spirit impresses the exceeding sinfulness of sin upon the soul, a sense of condemnation and guilt rests heavily upon us and we long to have this load lifted. Then the Spirit points us to Calvary. As we pour out our souls in repentance and confession, the condemnation rolls away. We experience the freedom Paul, the wretched, felt when he found deliverance in Christ Jesus. (Romans 7:24, 25.) That this sense of condemnation might not return, we are to "walk in the Spirit." "There is therefore now no condemnation to them which are in Christ Jesus, who walk not after the flesh, but after the Spirit." Romans 8:1.

Though God has provided a way whereby the righteous may be delivered in the judgment, He also "knoweth how . . . to reserve the unjust unto the day of judgment to be punished." (2 Peter 2:9.) The Holy Spirit earnestly and often pleads with sinners to forsake their evil ways and accept salvation. "The Holy Ghost saith, To day if ye will hear his voice, harden not your hearts." Hebrews 3:7, 8. The Pentecostal appeal of the Spirit sounds across the centuries. Would that it might reach the lost of every nation, kindred, tongue, and people: "Save yourselves from this untoward generation." Acts 2:40.

Guidance
by the Spirit of Truth

Long ago the prophet Jeremiah declared, "O Lord, I know that the way of man is not in himself: it is not in man that walketh to direct his steps." Jeremiah 10:23. Though man thinks highly of himself, he still needs guidance.

Our Lord was preeminently a teacher—"a teacher come from God," as Nicodemus addressed Him. (John 3:2.) Jesus, Himself the Truth, was the Teacher of truth. On one occasion Jesus said, "Ye shall know the truth, and the truth shall make you free." John 8:32.

But Jesus was not to be with His disciples long. He knew, moreover, that they would be in need of guidance to the end of time. Therefore, before His departure He spoke about His successor, "another Comforter" (John 14:16), "the Spirit of truth," One who would guide His followers "into all truth" (John 16:13). By Christ's own arrangement every member of His body, the church, may have the indwelling presence of His Spirit. Through this great and measureless gift the prophecy of Isaiah finds fulfillment: "All thy children shall be taught of the Lord." Isaiah 54:13.

Do these promises apply to the unconverted? Will the worldling have the Holy Spirit as an indwelling teacher? No, the Spirit's work for the unconverted is to convict them of sin and to lead them to accept the righteousness of Jesus. Only those who have had their sins pardoned through the merits of the shed blood of Jesus can know the indwelling presence of the Holy Spirit. A heart that has not been cleansed of its sins cannot be host to the Holy Guest. (John 14:17; Psalm 51:2, 10.)

Many both in and out of the church think they know Jesus, because they know so much about Him. But without the Holy Spirit no one can really know Jesus: "No man can say that Jesus is the Lord, but by the Holy Ghost." 1 Corinthians 12:3. For instance, to Peter's great confession, "Thou art the Christ, the Son of the living God," Christ replied, "Flesh and blood hath not revealed it unto thee, but my Father which is in heaven." Matthew 16:16, 17. No man can confess that Jesus is the Christ unless he receives this knowledge as a supernatural revelation.

61

The eyes of our understanding must be enlightened by "the spirit of wisdom and revelation." (Ephesians 1:17, 18.)

In fact, the entire Bible reveals or unveils Jesus Christ, and the Bible itself can be understood only as we welcome "the spirit of . . . revelation" into our hearts. Only the Spirit can make God's Word clear and plain. God has promised, "I will pour out my spirit unto you, I will make known my words unto you." Proverbs 1:23. By His Spirit God makes His words known. Only the Spirit of God can rightly interpret their true meaning, because the Holy Spirit knows better than anyone else what He meant when He inspired the Bible writers to write.

Why can't the unconverted understand the Bible? Because the love of sin constitutes a mental block that inhibits the grasping of spiritual truths.

Paul said, "Which things also we speak, not in the words which man's wisdom teacheth, but which the Holy Ghost teacheth; comparing spiritual things with spiritual. But the natural man receiveth not the things of the Spirit of God: for they are foolishness unto him: neither can he know them, because they are spiritually discerned." 1 Corinthians 2:13, 14.

Divine guidance calls for obedience. In the very process of obeying, the Holy Spirit purifies the soul. Peter remarked to one group, "Ye have purified your souls in obeying the truth through the Spirit." 1 Peter 1:22. The very purpose of the Spirit's presence is "sanctification . . . unto obedience." (1 Peter 1:2.)

The Sword
of the Spirit

How does the Holy Spirit guide men? What instruments does He use? Paul advised the church at Ephesus to "take . . . the sword of the Spirit, which is the word of God." (Ephesians 6:17.) This Sword of the Spirit exposes to the inner man his hidden propensities and underlying motives. "The word of God is quick, and powerful, and sharper than any twoedged sword, piercing even to the dividing asunder of soul and spirit, . . . and is a discerner of the thoughts and intents of the heart." Hebrews 4:12. It also promises victory to the Christian. The Apostle Paul said, "I commend you to God, and to the word of his grace, which is able to build you up, and to give you an inheritance among all them which are sanctified." Acts 20:32.

When you pick up your Bible, you hold a library of sixty-six books, yet they are one in spirit, for they have all been inspired by the Holy Spirit. During a period of 1,500 years the Holy Spirit used men from all walks of life, and at different times and in different places, to give us this wonderful library. Of whom did they speak? The Man of the Book is Christ Jesus. "To him give all the prophets witness." Acts 10:43. When Jesus once admonished His followers, "Search the scriptures," He added, "They . . . testify of me." John 5:39.

As truly as every dewdrop reflects the glory of the morning sun, so all the Bible reflects in some way the wondrous beauty of Jesus.

Other writers cannot be present when their books are read, but the Bible differs, for the Holy Bible is the living Word of God, and Christ by His Spirit draws near to those who read the Book with a desire to know and obey the truth. The Bible itself clearly teaches that the Holy Spirit inspired those who wrote this timeless volume. Peter declared, "Holy men of God spake as they were moved by the Holy Ghost." 2 Peter 1:21.

The inspiration of this Book differs in quality from that which prompts other writings. The Apostle Paul says, "Every Scripture is God-breathed." 2 Timothy 3:16, The Amplified Bible. There is life, then, in every word. It will accomplish everything for which it is sent. (Isaiah 55:11.) And what is its mission? It is "for doctrine, for reproof, for correction, for instruction in righteousness." (2 Timothy 3:16.) All Scripture is inspired by the Holy Spirit and is to be to our spiritual being as God's life-imparting breath.

Some do not understand God's Word, not because they cannot, but because they will not. They are, according to 2 Peter 3:5, willfully ignorant. Paul rebuked the dissidents who refused to accept the testimony of the holy prophets who had foretold Christ's ministry as a servant and His sacrifice as a sin offering. Notice his words, just as clear, as penetrating, and as true today as when they came from his prison in Rome: "Well spake the Holy Ghost by Esaias, . . . Go unto this people, and say, . . . Seeing ye shall see, and not perceive: . . . their eyes have they closed; lest they should see, . . . and understand with their heart, and should be converted." Acts 28:25-27.

The intellectually honest person can understand enough of God's Word to be converted. Only those who choose to close their eyes will be blind to truth. The old adage remains as true today as when first coined: "None [are] so blind as those that will not see." A loving and kind God provides opportunity to know His will, but He will never invade the will. Since God made man a free moral agent, He gives him liberty to make his own choice. According to the scripture just quoted, those who are willing to weigh the evidences will "understand with their heart." The Holy Bible speaks to all in a language that the heart can understand. The Bible speaks to you. As you read God's Book, His heart speaks to your heart. He delights to hold a heart-to-heart conversation with you. And you can understand Him if you really desire to. (Jeremiah 29:13.)

The Apostle Paul pointed out that Isaiah was not the source of what he wrote. (Acts 28:25-27.) He was but the mouthpiece of the Holy Ghost. The same Holy Spirit who spoke through Isaiah speaks today, not only through Isaiah but by the writings of all the holy prophets.

An incident took place at Cornelius's home as Peter preached that illustrates how the Holy Spirit speaks: "The Holy Ghost fell on all them which heard the word." Acts 10:44. This is the key. Would you have the Holy Spirit? Hear the Word! Do you want others to have the Holy Spirit? Let them hear the Word!

Inspired writers have called both the Bible and Christ the Word of God. Though not privileged as the disciples were to walk with the Master and to hear His voice, we may still hear Jesus speak to us today out of the pages of the Written Word even as He spoke orally to His disciples nearly twenty centuries ago. Jesus, "the truth" (John 14:6), has sent the Spirit of truth to minister the "word of truth" to our souls. There can never be any conflict or inconsistency or contradiction between the Spirit of truth and the Word of truth. Of His Successor, Jesus said, "He shall receive of mine, and shall shew it unto you." John 16:14. In other words, the Spirit of truth will direct those who will be guided to the very words in the Bible that Jesus would speak to them if He were personally with them.

As light flashes from God's Word upon your pathway, however, it becomes the special work of the Holy Spirit to prompt you to obey it, and the evidence that you are being led of the Spirit will be seen in your obedience. Any spirit that fails to harmonize with the Word of God, or any spirit that would have you acknowledge Bible truth but at the same time suggest to you that obedience is unnecessary is an unholy spirit.

Many chapters in the Bible such as Romans 3, Ephesians 2, and John 6 contain profound theology. Though the reasoning may often seem involved and difficult to grasp, the basic conclusions are simple. This is particularly true of the sixth chapter of John, in which the Master explains how the Holy Spirit's quickening presence permeated the very words He spoke: "It is the spirit that quickeneth; the flesh profiteth nothing: the words that I speak unto you, they are spirit, and they are life." John 6:63.

Jesus had just startled His hearers by offering His body as food and His blood as drink. Those who took Him literally, questioning the meaning of what He had said, "went back, and walked no more with him." (John 6:66.) By refusing to try to learn what He meant, they rejected Christ. Since it is the Holy Spirit in the Word of God that gives life, they rejected the

Holy Spirit, too. Jesus, seeing the crowds melt away, asked His disciples, "Will ye also go away?" Peter's answer shows that he had understood the meaning of Christ's words. "To whom shall we go?" he said; "thou hast the words of eternal life." (Verses 67, 68.) To reject Christ's Word is to reject life.

Even so, the Holy Spirit accompanies the reading of the Holy Word, giving life to the receiver—eternal life. Those who accept the Word and apply it in their daily life receive the benefits of Christ's broken body and spilled blood. These people will be raised in the resurrection of the just. Jesus is, indeed, the Living Bread because His Word provides bread for our spiritual nature. This concept should not be difficult for the spiritually minded to grasp, but we may not grasp its full importance in a moment. We must prayerfully contemplate this. One basic point should stand out: that God works through His Word to impart life, light, and power to the soul.

Thus the Holy Spirit employs the Holy Word to reach us just where we are, to get through to us, and to beget within us a spiritual life. Moreover, the Spirit of God uses the Word to sustain that spiritual life. "Man shall not live by bread alone, but by every word that proceedeth out of the mouth of God." Matthew 4:4. And what kind of life does the Spirit impart to those who live by God's Word? Peter says that God's "exceeding great and precious promises" are given to us that by these promises we might become "partakers of the divine nature." (2 Peter 1:4.)

Conscience–
Monitored by the Spirit

The tool used by the Holy Spirit in guiding the learning processes is the Word of God. He uses another tool, the conscience, in providing guidance in the daily actions.

While the indwelling Spirit of God works with the whole man, we feel His influence especially in the conscience. Many imagine that they can just naturally know the difference between good and evil, right and wrong. They feel that they should follow their own desires. But may we safely follow the inclinations of our hearts? Proverbs 28:26 declares, "He that trusteth in his own heart is a fool." And Jeremiah 17:9 insists, "The heart is deceitful above all things, and desperately wicked." Now, if we can't be sure we are doing right when we are doing what we think is right, and we can't be sure we are doing right when we follow the dictates of our own heart, how can we ever be sure?

We often hear the expression, "Let your conscience be your guide." But the conscience not enlightened by the Holy Spirit can be a power for evil. Heathen women have in obedience to conscience offered their babies to their gods. In spite of the fact that they have followed an inner urge, such actions do not stem from the Holy Spirit.

Conscience belongs to the natural man and must be taught of God. Conscience is that within a man which tells him, "Do so and so." The conscience gives a sense of well-being to a man when he obeys and distress when he disobeys. But conscience of itself does not tell what is right. Conscience must be educated in order to be a true guide.

God has ordained that conscience serve as man's moral regulator, but conscience itself must be regulated. Watches which regulate time for us must first be regulated themselves. So man's conscience must be regulated, or enlightened, by the Holy Spirit. How is this to be done? The special means which the Holy Spirit uses to enlighten the conscience is the Word of God. The promptings of the conscience must be regulated by the Holy Word. A conscience divinely enlightened by the Word of God can safely guide and serve as a true guardian of the soul. Obedience to such a conscience assures one of peace of mind now and a life in heaven at last.

But if we continually rebuff conscience, if we don't allow it to prompt us to do what is right, it will not only cease to monitor our acts, but will eventually justify our doing wrong. It will excuse and explain away sin by such sinister suggestions as "Everybody's doing it," "It's only a white lie," and "There's nothing wrong if you don't get caught." What is the result? Conscience becomes like the sheep dog which rends and devours instead of defending the sheep, like a policeman who actually burglarizes the homes of the people on his beat instead of protecting them, like a judge who accepts bribes and perverts justice instead of upholding the law. When a man's conscience begins to excuse his sins, he may know that he has a traitor within his soul.

To what lengths will an evil conscience lead a man? Jesus warned His disciples that there would be zealous people so deceived in their ideas of right and wrong that they would even imagine that they were serving God when murdering Christ's followers. (John 16:2.)

Paul constantly aimed to have a good conscience. "Herein do I exercise myself, to have always a conscience void of offense toward God, and toward men." Acts 24:16.

The question of primary importance is, How can we have an enlightened conscience—a conscience taught of God? Paul said, "I say the truth in Christ, I lie not, my conscience also bearing me witness in

71

the Holy Ghost." Romans 9:1. How did Paul know he told the truth, that he had no sham, no hypocrisy, and no subterfuge within his soul? Because he had the inner witness of the Holy Spirit. When we have the approval of conscience, we should do what it tells us to do. But conscience cannot tell us what is right except as it is enlightened by the Spirit of truth. And remember, the Spirit of truth and the Word of truth will always agree. Conscience enlightened by the Word of God and influenced by the Holy Spirit becomes the voice of God to the soul.

When the "inner you" (which God holds responsible for every decision regarding morals) chooses to obey a conscience taught by the Holy Spirit and says, "I will do right," then God works with you to strengthen your will in carrying out that which you have determined to do. (Philippians 2:13.) God supplies the omnipotent power of the Spirit to help you carry out good resolutions.

Each man will be judged by the kind of conscience he has developed in this life. A good conscience makes a good man, a bad conscience a bad man. But whether good or bad, the kind of conscience one has results from one's own choosing.

Three phrases describe the phases of the takeover of the conscience by an unholy spirit. Titus 1:15 speaks of a defiled conscience, one that has been compromised and imposed upon; Hebrews 10:22, an evil conscience, one so warped and twisted that it excuses and condones sin; and 1 Timothy 4:2, a seared conscience, one so scarred by sin that it cannot be impressed by the Holy Spirit.

But no one needs to have an evil conscience. The gospel ultimately aims at having a good conscience. Hebrews 9:14 asks, "How much more shall the blood of Christ, who through the eternal Spirit offered himself without spot to God, purge your conscience from dead works to serve the living God?" The grand objective of Christ's crucifixion is that our consciences be purged from all taint of evil, all compromise with sin. Nothing stands more invincible than a conscience that acknowledges the sovereignty of the Holy Spirit. The union of the divine with the human in the conscience brings power—invincible power.

Spiritual Stature

Heaven measures people not by their bank accounts, their popularity ratings, or their university degrees. Moral stature alone counts.

After Paul received a vision of Jesus Christ which completely changed his life, he said, "For me to live is Christ." Philippians 1:21. Christianity, for him, consisted not in rituals, forms, and ceremonies, projects, plans, and programs, but in "Christ." Paul, though small of stature, cast a long shadow across the centuries. He "determined not to know any thing . . . save Jesus Christ, and him crucified" and to preach Him "in demonstration of the Spirit and of power." (1 Corinthians 2:2, 4.)

Paul's goal should be ours. Christlikeness should

be our constant aim in life. Paul said, "This one thing I do, forgetting those things which are behind, and reaching forth unto those things which are before, I press toward the mark for the prize of the high calling of God in Christ Jesus." Philippians 3:13, 14.

We too should not only receive Christ, but we should also grow in Him. "As many as received him, to them gave he power to become the sons of God." John 1:12. The words "power to become" indicate a growing, developing, continuing experience; and it is "for the perfecting of the saints" that the gifts of the Spirit were bestowed "till we all come . . . unto a perfect man, unto the measure of the stature of the fulness of Christ." (Ephesians 4:8-13.) God wants us to grow up, to become adults, to reach spiritual maturity.

As Christians we will have trials and temptations, difficulties and hardships, interspersed with heart satisfactions and holy joys. But all along, those who have the Spirit of God will have the inner assurance that they are sons and daughters of God. "For as many as are led by the Spirit of God, they are the sons of God." Romans 8:14.

The Spirit of God will never lead us into situations that will overwhelm us. The prophet Isaiah declared, "When the enemy shall come in like a flood, the Spirit of the Lord shall lift up a standard against him." Isaiah 59:19. Today the tidal wave of sin has risen to flood stage, ready to engulf the world, but this text says that at such a time the Spirit of the Lord will raise a standard in opposition. Not by compromising with sin nor by lowering the standards of the church to accommodate man in his fallen state, but by exalting the standard of the Spirit will Satan be defeated.

The world presents standards utterly unacceptable to the Christian. Some people seem to think that if they are clever, they don't need to be righteous. Their philosophy is, If you are smart enough to get away with it, anything is all right.

Others feel that they can't go wrong if they go with the crowd. They pass off their inconsistencies with a glib "Everybody's doing it." They defend their racy language, smutty stories, personality clashes, scanty attire, immodest behavior, and bold intemperance with an appeal to "It's the fashion" or "I don't want to be an oddball." These fear what others may think about them more than what God thinks about them. But God expressly commands, "Thou shalt not follow a multitude to do evil." Exodus 23:2. Suppose everybody in the world voted to keep Wednesday as the Sabbath. Would that change God? Can God be outvoted? Let the Bible answer: "What if some did not believe? shall their unbelief make the faith of God without effect? God forbid: yea, let God be true, but every man a liar." Romans 3:3, 4.

What man thinks doesn't count anyway, for God measures His people. He is measuring us now. Are we ready to face the verdict of the judgment? The word has gone forth, "Rise, and measure the temple of God, and the altar, and them that worship therein." Revelation 11:1.

When the children of Israel became "chummy" with the heathen peoples around them, they began to clamor for a king "that we . . . may be like all the nations." (1 Samuel 8:20.) Why were they so infatuated with the governments about them? It is a sociological law that people tend to be like those whose company they enjoy.

When reprimanding King Jehoshaphat, the Old Testament prophet Jehu said, "Shouldest thou help the ungodly, and love them that hate the Lord?" 2 Chronicles 19:2.

No one will ever be taller than his ideals as expressed in his friendships. God wants us to make Jesus Christ our Friend and Pattern. When the Spirit of God lifts a standard against the enemy, He points us to Jesus, for it is the Spirit's special work to "glorify" our Lord. (John 16:14.) "Looking unto Jesus the author and finisher of our faith" (Hebrews 12: 2), we will become more and more like Him. The Spirit helps us develop an image likeness of our Lord. "We all, with open face beholding as in a glass the glory of the Lord, are changed into the same image from glory to glory even as by the Spirit of the Lord." 2 Corinthians 3:18.

The Spirit Presents
the Standard of the Judgment

Self-made standards must be continually changed and adjusted to meet the outcroppings of new weaknesses in our fallen nature. It is easy to understand why there are so many mixed-up people in the world. God does not leave us to ourselves to decide what is right or wrong. We are not to be law-makers, but law keepers. "The Lord is our lawgiver, the Lord is our king." Isaiah 33:22. He has given us a moral code of behavior, short, authoritative, and comprehensive—the Ten Commandments. This is the standard of the judgment. We shall be judged by this law as lived out in the life of Jesus. There can be no judgment without a law or standard of judgment. And of course there could be no such thing as sin or righteousness without a law or standard. Paul said, "Where no law is, there is no transgression." "Sin is not imputed when there is no law." Romans 4:15; 5:13. And John said, "Sin is the transgression of the law." 1 John 3:4. Without law there could be no government, and without government there would be no Ruler; the universe would then be chaos, not a cosmos.

"Bad laws" have been enacted by earthly legislative bodies because these groups have favored one segment of society above another. Any law that fails to protect the rights of minority groups is tyrannical, whether that law be enacted by a one-man dictatorship or by a majority dictatorship. But "the law of the Lord is perfect." (Psalm 19:7.) "The law is holy, and the commandment holy, and just, and good," and "we know that the law is spiritual." (Romans 7:12, 14.) "Thy law is truth," and "all his commandments are sure. They stand fast for ever and ever." (Psalms 119:142; 111:7, 8.)

God has given to us a spiritual law, a revelation of His character. All that God is, His law is. The law reflects His love, mercy, goodness, justice, creative power. Some, ignorantly, have called God's law a "yoke of bondage," but the Bible speaks of it as "the perfect law of liberty." (James 1:25.)

Solomon admonished all to observe the standard by which they will be judged: "Let us hear the conclusion of the whole matter: Fear God, and keep his commandments: for this is the whole duty of man.

For God shall bring every work into judgment, with every secret thing, whether it be good, or whether it be evil." Ecclesiastes 12:13, 14. The judgment spoken of here concerns good and evil; it deals with secret things, the thoughts, motives, attitudes, and intents of the heart.

Man needs more than a written code. He needs a demonstration of what it means to keep the law through the indwelling power of the Spirit. Christ's life provides such an example of perfect obedience. He came to our planet, as Isaiah said, to "magnify the law, and make it honourable." (Isaiah 42:21.)

In the Sermon on the Mount, Christ said, "Think not that I am come to destroy the law." Matthew 5: 17. Jesus lived out the Ten Commandments through the Spirit. The law of God was in His heart. He could honestly say, "I delight to do thy will, O my God: yea, thy law is within my heart." Psalm 40:8. As His earthly life drew to a close, He declared, "I have kept my Father's commandments, and abide in his love." John 15:10.

The Holy Spirit, who enabled Christ to keep the law, will write the law upon the tables of our hearts. The Apostle Paul says, "Ye are manifestly declared to be the epistle of Christ, . . . written not with ink, but with the Spirit of the living God; not in tables of stone, but in fleshy tables of the heart." 2 Corinthians 3:3.

Mere obedience to the form or letter of the law results only in death, "but the spirit giveth life."

When the Holy Spirit directs our actions, He fills the letter with life. (Verse 6.) The Spirit-filled obey as a matter of privilege rather than of obligation. Oh, that we might have the more glorious "ministration of the spirit"! (Verse 8.) God describes those who "know" or experience righteousness as "the people in whose heart is my law." (Isaiah 51:7.)

No one can truly accept Christ and not accept His Spirit. Both the Holy Man and the Holy Spirit magnify the law of God. What the Spirit did in Christ He is to do in every believer who accepts Christ.

Many fail here. They want the benefits of Christ's death, but they do not accept the Spirit by which He lived. They want forgiveness for, but not victory over, sin. Everyone needs to understand two terms: (1) "The Spirit in Christ" refers to what the Spirit did in our Lord during His life on earth. (2) "Christ in us" refers to what the Spirit does in us so that we might duplicate His life. Paul clearly stated this: "The law of the Spirit of life *in Christ Jesus* hath made me free from the law of sin and death." "That the righteousness of the law might be fulfilled *in us,* who walk not after the flesh, but after the Spirit." Romans 8:2, 4.

God "hath appointed a day in the which he will judge the world in righteousness by that man." (Acts 17:31.) God will judge us according to the law as lived out "by that man." The standard of the judgment is *that Man.* Christ obeyed by the Spirit, and so it may be with us.

"To Be Spiritually Minded Is Life"

"I'd rather do a hard day's work in the field with my husband than to have to think for half an hour," was the honest confession of a farmer's wife as she watched a minister preparing for his evening sermon. Most people do not think for five minutes a day. They lead only mechanical lives—going and coming, getting and spending.

Intense worldliness has enslaved men's minds. Secularism has blunted interest in things spiritual. Never were men so carnally minded. But "to be carnally minded is death." (Romans 8:6.) A world intoxicated with materialism remains unaware of its danger. Our thought patterns must be changed if we would meet the standards of the Spirit. We need the presiding power of the Holy Spirit to give us the mind of Christ.

Solomon said of man, "As he thinketh in his heart, so is he." Proverbs 23:7. Those who are born again will have a change of heart, a change of mind. There's a good reason why the Bible says, "Let this mind be in you, which was also in Christ Jesus." Philippians 2:5. We do not naturally have such a mind. Those who would have the mind of Christ must be willing to think His thoughts after Him. As we do this, we will be of one mind, for we will think together and think alike.

Some believe we settle the final issues of the inner conflict between right and wrong solely on the basis of our desires, but while desire may make strong appeals, God purposes that desire should always be under the control of the will. It is the mind that wills to do things. The mind ponders relationships and accepts or rejects. The mind resolves the elemental issues of life—issues that affect our eternal destiny. What a man thinks determines what he is.

Men may have either of two kinds of minds. Paul said, "For to be carnally minded is death; but to be spiritually minded is life and peace." Romans 8:6. Here Paul contrasted two very different kinds of minds. To think as a worldling thinks can only eventuate in death, while to think as a converted person thinks offers peace and eternal life. He who has the mind of the Spirit will meet the standards of the Spirit. Both kinds of minds, the carnal and the spiritual, produce thoughts. How, then, do they differ? "The carnal mind is enmity against God: for it is not subject to the law of God, neither indeed can be." Romans 8:7. Here is the answer! "The carnal mind is enmity," that is to say, at war with God. Over what? Over the law.

And this is the core of the problem. The carnal mind simply refuses subjection to God's law. In plain language, a perpetual antagonism, or fierce resentment, toward the law dwells in the carnal mind. The requirements of the law make the carnal man fighting mad. Its restraints annoy him, and its demands irk him. When the law says "Don't" to his desires, the carnal nature within rises up in rebellion to defy God's "Thou shalt not." And even should he try to obey the law, he couldn't, for it is contrary to his very nature. (Galatians 5:17.) But the new covenant promise given by God offers a brighter picture. God says, "I will put my laws into their mind, and write them in their hearts." Hebrews 8:10. By the impartation of His Spirit God plants His laws in the minds of those He has regenerated.

"I will put my spirit within you, and cause you to walk in my statutes, and ye shall keep my judgments, and do them." Ezekiel 36:27. God assures us that the Holy Spirit will supply all the power necessary for obedience. If you believe God, He will cause you to keep and do His law. Surely He will do in you what He has promised to do in you and what He is now doing in others.

84

The Book of Romans stands out as one of the clearest expositions of "righteousness by faith." Paul reaches the climax of his reasoning in Romans 8:4: "That the righteousness of the law might be fulfilled in us, who walk not after the flesh, but after the Spirit." Paul concluded that the grand purpose of Christ's death goes beyond forgiveness for past sins and beyond the imputing of Christ's righteousness to all who accept His vicarious death. All who have accepted Christ are to live as Christ lived and overcome temptation as He overcame. The righteousness of the law is to be fulfilled in us. How? By the Holy Spirit.

Christ offers us a twofold gift. First, He puts to our account His perfect righteousness when we accept Him by faith. That is righteousness for us, or righteousness credited to us. Those who are born again are counted righteous. Second, when we become His children, He writes His law in our hearts by the impartation of His Holy Spirit. It is in obedience that the righteousness of the law is fulfilled in us.

Before anyone can keep the law, he must first change his mind regarding the law. Reception of the Holy Spirit changes our minds, and we now accept the law as "holy, and just, and good." "To be spiritually minded is life and peace." This imparting of power by the Holy Spirit for living out the law is imparted righteousness, or sanctification. And by accepting this we meet the requirements of the Spirit.

The Fruits
of the Spirit

Unbelievers have little concern for what the Christian believes—they are far more interested in the fruitage of his faith. Does your faith make you easy to get along with? generously dispositioned? selflessly concerned for others? Does your love for Jesus keep you good-natured? sweet-tempered? cheerful? Said the Master, "By this shall all men know that ye are my disciples, if ye have love one to another." John 13:35.

At another time Christ declared of those who professed to be religious, "By their fruits ye shall know them." Matthew 7:20. Not by certain signs or manifestations are Christ's followers to be known, but by their fruits. Christ warned His followers to beware of false prophets, false tongues, false healings, and false signs, because Satan can easily counterfeit. God earnestly warns us to beware of Satan's masquerades: "The Spirit speaketh expressly, that in the latter times some shall depart from the faith, giving heed to seducing spirits, and doctrines of devils; speaking lies in hypocrisy; having their conscience seared with a hot iron." 1 Timothy 4:1, 2.

God has indeed given various gifts or manifestations of the Spirit, but He has made it clear that these are to be tested; they are not to be themselves the test. Christ made the fruits of the Spirit the all-important test. The fruit we bear tells the world whether we have enthroned the carnal nature in our hearts or the Spirit of Christ, whether we have allowed ourselves to be controlled by an unholy spirit or by the Holy Spirit.

To say that one is controlled by the Holy Spirit is not to say that there is no more conflict with sin. Galatians 5:17 describes the conflict that will exist as long as we are mortal: "The flesh lusteth against the Spirit, and the Spirit against the flesh: and these are contrary the one to the other." The world may not be able to see the struggle going on in the heart, but the world can see who is winning the battle by the way we behave. The Christian may fall occasionally, but he regrets his un-Christlike acts and endeavors to overcome.

The fruit of the Spirit, according to Galatians 5:22, 23, is "love, joy, peace, longsuffering, gentleness, goodness, faith, meekness, temperance." The Holy Spirit blesses us with all these attributes. Love heads the list. At creation God endowed man with His own love; but when Adam sinned, his capacities to love became limited—he could not love God with all his heart or his neighbor as himself. Those who are born of the Spirit experience that original love, a love beyond anything that the unconverted soul could know—God's kind of love.

We naturally love those who love us, but Jesus told His disciples to love those who did not love them. (Matthew 5:44-48.) True love, He said, would go even so far as to die for a friend. (John 15:13.) Christ had this kind of love and more, for "while we were yet sinners, Christ died for us." (Romans 5:8.)

The followers of Jesus must love with a more than natural love, for Jesus commanded them to love "*as* I have loved you." (John 13:34.)

How can man ever hope to have a love that human beings do not naturally possess? The Bible provides an answer: "The love of God is shed abroad in our hearts by the Holy Ghost which is given unto us." Romans 5:5. God manifests His love to us by the Holy Spirit, which testifies of Christ; and as we behold His love, we are changed. The Holy Spirit gives us the very same kind of love that dwells in the heart of God. But it is ours only as we use it.

We cannot grasp the full meaning of the love of God. The Apostle Paul after exhausting the heights and depths, the lengths and breadths, of language, exclaimed that the love of Christ "passeth knowledge." (Ephesians 3:16-19.) We do not have to understand God's love to accept it and appreciate it. The heart can accept what the mind cannot comprehend.

Every Christian can know the love of God, and in his daily life reveal that love. His life may become a sermon for all to see. All of the fruits of the Spirit are to be beautifully blended in the lives of Christians. Their lives will not attract attention to themselves, but will ever point to Jesus.

"There is no fear in love, but perfect love casteth out fear." 1 John 4:18. Those who are responsive to the love of the Spirit will "love in the Spirit." (Colossians 1:8.) The "love of the Spirit" contagiously inspires courage. Many a person has been lifted above his doubts and fears by the "spirit . . . of love" (2 Timothy 1:7) revealed in the unselfish acts of another's life.

Joy in the
Holy Spirit

Why does the Christian seem to have a different kind of happiness than others? Conversion does not alter his physical body, the color of his eyes, or the shape of his nose. His financial standing isn't changed. Yet his attitudes, interests, and desires are different. He has a new way of life and a new kind of joy. There is no dictionary definition for this kind of joy. Kaleidoscopic, with many facets, it simply has to be experienced to be appreciated. When David portrayed Christ, he said, "God . . . hath anointed thee with the oil of gladness above thy fellows." Psalm 45:7. Everyone who accepts Christ becomes anointed with the same "oil of gladness."

A contagion of joy surrounds true Christians!

After Pentecost, wherever the disciples carried the message of redeeming love, irrepressible joy sprang up. The Spirit of God so filled the disciples that they actually rejoiced that they should be found worthy of suffering for Christ's sake. (Acts 5:41.) In this they resembled their Master "who for the joy that was set before him endured the cross." (Hebrews 12:2.) For the encouragement of the church to the end of time Peter wrote, "If ye be reproached for the name of Christ, happy are ye; for the spirit of glory and of God resteth upon you." 1 Peter 4:14.

The fifth book in the New Testament called The Acts of the Apostles could well have been called The Book of Joy, for as the disciples preached Christ in the power of the Spirit, they filled hearts and homes and whole cities with heavenly joy. When Philip preached Christ in Samaria, the Sacred Record says, "there was great joy in that city." (Acts 8:8.) And speaking of the Gentile converts who took their stand in Antioch of Pisidia, the Bible says, "The disciples were filled with joy, and with the Holy Ghost." Acts 13:52. Joy invariably accompanies the operations of the Holy Ghost.

In times like these when so much feuding and fighting divides homes and neighborhoods, churches and nations, we need the fresh winds of the Holy Spirit to breathe upon us heavenly joy. If we have the Holy Spirit, then we will count trials and temptations for Christ's sake a joy! (James 1:2.) In this twilight hour of earth's history which precedes Christ's actual coming in the clouds of glory, we need a new revelation of the joy that filled and overflowed the heart of Christ, the happiest Man that ever lived.

Paul described God's kingdom as "righteousness, and peace, and joy in the Holy Ghost." (Romans 14: 17.) There must be joy where God says there is joy. And God says there is joy in the Holy Ghost. How do we receive this joy? Paul said, "Now the God of hope fill you with all joy and peace in believing, that ye may abound in hope, through the power of the Holy Ghost." Romans 15:13. How do we get "all joy"? By believing. What is the source of "all joy"? "The power of the Holy Ghost." The presence of the Holy Spirit in the soul brings health-giving, life-giving joy.

Can the mentally ill and the emotionally disturbed experience all joy and peace? Indeed, God specializes in what man calls hard cases and impossible situations! Is there hope for the irritable and nervous? Of course. For the gambler and alcoholic? Surely! For the philanderer and the adulteress? Yes!

God wants His children to be happy. Paul's admonition in Philippians 4:4 speaks to every Christian: "Rejoice in the Lord alway: and again I say, Rejoice." We may find the same happiness Jesus had just where He found it. Jesus "rejoiced in the Holy Spirit." (Luke 10:21, R.S.V.) Weymouth translates, "Jesus was filled by the Holy Spirit with rapturous joy."

"Joy unspeakable and full of glory" (1 Peter

1:8) awaits you if you will open your heart wide to the Holy Spirit. Begin today to obey the inner promptings of the Spirit by doing those things you know the Spirit would have you do. You will find joy in reading your Bible, in prayer, in telling someone else about your faith in Jesus. You may find inner satisfaction in being kind, thoughtful, and considerate; in giving help to the needy, encouragement to the downhearted, and love to the lonely.

Praying in the Spirit

Sooner or later, every soul comes face to face with the stark reality that life is nothing without Christ. Need awakens desire, and desire opens the way for prayer. When the Holy Spirit exposes your undone condition, He doesn't stop there, but He also prompts you to pray for help.

The Holy Spirit even offers to help you pray. Zechariah 12:10 says, "I will pour upon the house of David . . . the spirit of grace and of supplications: and they shall look upon me whom they have pierced." The Holy Spirit arouses in you an attitude of supplication as He takes you into the presence of the One who was pierced for your sake on the cross.

God immediately answered the prayer of the poor

publican, "God be merciful to me a sinner." Luke 18:13. Every sinner can pray that prayer and know that it will be answered. But too often we do not persist in prayer as we should. (Romans 12:12.) Many church members pray as little as nonchurch members. They fret and stew and worry with their shortcomings, but they do not pray about them. When prompted to pray, they stifle the inner urge. Thus the person who refuses to pray actually quenches the Spirit. Prayerlessness will eventually lead to spiritual suicide. Only he who doesn't pray will commit the "unpardonable sin." Every blessing received should prompt us to praise God in prayer. How can God give us greater blessings if we do not appreciate those already given?

Those who are not sensitive enough to the Holy Spirit's promptings to pray can never expect to be filled with the Spirit. God pours "the spirit of grace and of supplications" upon us that we might pray. Without the Spirit's help no one can pray an acceptable prayer. Paul declared, "I will pray with the spirit, and I will pray with the understanding also." 1 Corinthians 14:15. And Jude spoke of "praying in the Holy Ghost." (Jude 20.) God wants us to *pray* our prayers, not just *say* our prayers. We should be "praying always with all prayer and supplication in the Spirit." (Ephesians 6:18.) Praying in the Spirit means putting heart and soul into our requests—not forgetting, of course, to ask in faith and according to God's will.

In prayer it is our privilege to know "the fellowship of the Spirit," and "the communion of the Holy Ghost." We may become better acquainted with God by prayer than in any other way, especially when prayer takes the form of conversation. After telling God about our joys and needs, we should then listen to what the Spirit has to say to us.

Since the Holy Spirit imparts the urge to pray, our response should be to pray when so impressed. One reason for the spiritual poverty which abounds is that there is so little asking. James said, "Ye have not, because ye ask not." James 4:2. So start asking! But asking isn't enough—we must also ask aright. James pointed out, "Ye ask amiss, that ye may consume it upon your lusts." Verse 3. Our heavenly Father seeks to draw us to His great heart of love, to encourage us not to go farther away from Him.

As we pray, the Spirit may remind us of some neglected duty. Christ admonished, "When ye stand praying, forgive, if ye have ought against any." Mark 11:25. Then, too, we should cultivate pleasant home relations "that your prayers be not hindered." (1 Peter 3:7.) Concerning those who ask not in faith James declared, "Let not that man think that he shall receive anything of the Lord." (James 1:5-7.) From Christ's lips we have this promise: "What things soever ye desire, when ye pray, believe that ye receive them, and ye shall have them." Mark 11:24.

How shall we pray? "Always" (Luke 18:1), "labouring fervently" (Colossians 4:12), "without ceasing" (1 Thessalonians 5:17). Our capacities to receive and capabilities to use God's blessings will increase as we pray. When we pray in Christ's name and for His sake, we will realize the promise of John 15:7, "If ye abide in me, and my words abide in you, ye shall ask what ye will, and it shall be done unto you." Abiding in Christ plays an important role in the divine science of prayer.

In our prayers we should state our needs simply, for the Holy Spirit will translate our desires into the language of heaven and present them at the throne of grace with an eloquence that no human being can know—yes, "with groanings which cannot be uttered." (Romans 8:26.)

To whom should we pray? "For through him [that is, Jesus] we both have access by one Spirit unto the Father." Ephesians 2:18. In other words, a correct form of prayer is by the Spirit through the Son unto the Father.

What does the Bible urge us to pray for? Christ said, "Ask, and it shall be given you; seek, and ye shall find; knock, and it shall be opened unto you. For every one that asketh receiveth; and he that seeketh findeth; and to him that knocketh it shall be opened. If a son shall ask bread of any of you that is a father, will he give him a stone? or if he ask a fish, will he for a fish give him a serpent? or if he shall ask an egg, will he offer him a scorpion? If ye then, being evil, know how to give good gifts unto your children: how much more shall your heavenly Father

7

give the Holy Spirit to them that ask him?" Luke 11:9-13.

In these few verses Christ used the word *ask* or its equivalent ten times. Asking is a positive condition for receiving the Holy Spirit. Those who have not enough interest to pray for the Spirit disqualify themselves to receive Him. No one would appreciate this wonderful gift if he received it without asking for it. He would imagine that he could use the Spirit instead of letting the Spirit use him. God has no reluctance to answer our prayers for the Holy Spirit. Christ's death in a sense had one goal in mind: that His disciples might have the Holy Spirit in all His fullness. Christ gives us a measure of the Spirit to prompt us to pray for more of the Spirit. He wants us to desire a large infilling of the Spirit. This gift of gifts comprehends all other blessings.

It is not the quantity of our prayers that Heaven respects; nor our eloquence, no matter how flowery our language; nor our arguments, no matter how logically we present our requests; nor the time we spend in them. Rather it is our yearning, our heart cry for cleansing, and the sincerity which prompts our prayer that Heaven recognizes. God will never disappoint the soul that in sincerity and faith asks for the Holy Spirit.

He who prays with the Spirit, in the Spirit, by the Spirit, and for the Spirit is responding to the promptings of the Spirit. God answers such a prayer, for the Spirit Himself will present that request before the throne of God with groanings which cannot be uttered. God earnestly entreats us to pray, to pray without ceasing, and to pray especially for the outpouring of the Spirit.

Witness–
Empowered by the Spirit

He who grows in the Holy Spirit will witness of Christ. Just before His ascension Jesus said, "Ye shall receive power, after that the Holy Ghost is come upon you: and ye shall be witnesses unto me both in Jerusalem, and in all Judaea, and in Samaria, and unto the uttermost part of the earth." Acts 1:8. The power Jesus promised the disciples was especially for witnessing, and this power was to be personally and continuously communicated to them by the Holy Spirit.

Christ's victory while on this earth was twofold: He conquered sin and He conquered death. In fact, only His victory over sin made possible His victory over death. And His victory over sin would have been impossible even for the Son of God without the Holy Spirit.

Christ's victory over every conceivable temptation settles the question as to whether man aided by the Holy Spirit can obey God. In Christ's victory, according to Romans 8:3, our Lord "condemned sin in the flesh."

Did Christ fulfill His promise that the Holy Spirit would come upon the disciples and give them power to witness? In the midst of his sermon on the day of Pentecost Peter declared, "This Jesus hath God raised up, whereof we all are witnesses." Acts 2:32. On that day 120 testified of the resurrected Christ. They had felt within their souls "the power of his resurrection" (victory over sin) and could testify to what they had both seen and experienced. (Philippians 3:10.) Luke described the event in these words: "With great power gave the apostles witness of the resurrection: . . . and great grace was upon them all." Acts 4:33.

"Ye shall be witnesses"! A witness has no second-hand hearsay report to give; he can tell only what he has actually seen and felt. We must know the resurrection power in our lives. A witness not only has something to say, but he says it.

Some want power and yet have no story to tell. They have a sickly Laodicean experience which cheers no one and discourages many. (Revelation 3:14-20.) To listen to their lifeless testimonies sorely tries even the saints. The shout of victory needs to be heard throughout the camp. Let those who have not had an experience in overcoming sin seek first for overcoming power in their lives before trying to be missionary witnesses.

Several months before Jesus' death, His disciples upon returning from a missionary tour told Him of their experiences in meeting the people. Why, they had even cast out devils! Jesus, however, cautioned that miracles were secondary, that a Christian experience was of first importance. Then He made them a promise: "I give unto you power . . . over all the power of the enemy." Luke 10:19. Yes, Jesus has promised power to His followers—power over power; more than that, power over all the power of the enemy.

Does Jesus really have this power to give? After His resurrection "Jesus came and spake unto them, saying, All power is given unto me in heaven and in earth." Matthew 28:18. If we have Jesus, we have all power—all the power we can use to His honor and glory.

Peter said of Jesus, He was "put to death in the flesh, but quickened by the Spirit." (1 Peter 3:18.) Thus Jesus was "declared to be the Son of God with power, according to the spirit of holiness, by the resurrection from the dead." (Romans 1:4.) Christ's resurrection demonstrated the power of the Spirit over death. Thus His resurrection makes certain a resurrection for every soul that trusts in Him. The power that operated to bring Jesus from the grave will bring us from the grave.

The same Spirit that put life into our bodies in the beginning will put life into them in the resurrection. The vision of dry bones recorded in Ezekiel 37 plainly teaches this. The prophet beheld the dead recreated but without life; then "breath came into them, and they lived." (Verse 10.) Next the Lord spoke, saying, "When I have opened your graves, O my people, . . . and shall put my spirit in you, and ye shall live, . . . then shall ye know that I the Lord have spoken it, and performed it." Verses 13, 14.

The disciples who witnessed to Christ's resurrection had themselves died to sin and experienced the resurrection power of the Holy Spirit, which enabled them to walk in newness of life. Christ has given us the symbol of baptism to reenact His death, burial, and resurrection. "We are buried with him . . . into death," that is, we reckon ourselves dead unto sin, and we are raised up to "walk in newness of life," that is, to live a new life empowered by the Spirit. (Romans 6:4-6.) Christ calls all His disciples to be witnesses to His resurrection, for in that act of victory Christ has demonstrated the full and complete power of the Holy Spirit. And only as we accept that victory as ours can we have power for witnessing.

The Sanctuary—
A Teaching Institution

The sanctuary which God had the ancient Israelites build portrayed the plan of salvation in its furnishings and services.

God used symbolic ritualism to teach essential truths to the illiterate Israelites, lately liberated from Egyptian bondage. Nehemiah, when recounting God's mercies to Israel at Sinai, said, "Thou gavest also thy good spirit to instruct them." Nehemiah 9:20.

God loved Israel. He longed for a closer, more intimate relationship with them. So He charged Moses, saying, "Let them make me a sanctuary; that I may dwell among them" (Exodus 25:8)—not only in their midst, but also within each one of them—

because all who experienced by faith what the sanctuary services portrayed were to be indwelt by God (2 Corinthians 6:16).

Concerning the sanctuary and its furnishings God admonished Moses, "Look that thou make them after their pattern, which was shewed thee in the mount." Exodus 25:40. God desired the children of Israel to understand that the sanctuary they were to build was but a miniature likeness of a much greater sanctuary. As the writer of the Book of Hebrews later pointed out, the ceremonies of the earthly tabernacle were to "serve unto the example and shadow of heavenly things." (Hebrews 8:1-5.)

Even in the building of the sanctuary the Holy Spirit held general superintendency. "The Lord spake unto Moses, saying, See, I have called by name Bezaleel: . . . and I have filled him with the spirit of God. . . . And in the hearts of all that are wise hearted I have put wisdom, that they may make all that I have commanded thee." Exodus 31:1-6.

The sanctuary and later its expanded counterpart, the Temple, portrayed the gospel in figures, types, and symbols. David wrote, "Thy way, O God, is in the sanctuary." Psalm 77:13. "They have seen thy goings, O God; even the goings of my God, my King, in the sanctuary." Psalm 68:24.

The Holy Spirit has interpreted to Israel and the Christian church the meaning of the sanctuary ceremonies. The expression "the Holy Ghost this signifying," used in Hebrews 9:1-8 to show that the old covenant sanctuary is a type of the new covenant sanctuary in heaven, makes this point clear. Most of the worship in the sanctuary consisted of prayers performed and sermons enacted. The Holy Spirit worked through the priests to teach and interpret the spiritual significance of the various ceremonies—to show how they served as *aids to faith* and helped to explain such basic truths as the love of God, the holiness of God's law, the awfulness of sin, Christ's atonement, justification, sanctification, the judgment, and the blended justice and mercy of God.

The sanctuary services held three mysteries or truths which could be known only by revelation: (1) the mystery of the altar, (2) the mystery of the holy place, and (3) the mystery of the most holy place.

The Altar: Every animal sacrifice offered upon the brazen altar prefigured Christ's death and the forgiveness which it made available. Man estranged by sin could be reconciled to God only at this altar. First, the Holy Spirit aroused the sinner to see something of the sacredness of God's holy law and the awfulness of his transgression. As a moral culprit the sinner realized that he could never find peace within except as God came into his heart and imparted His peace to him. Then the Spirit prompted the penitent sinner to take the sacrifice required to the altar, place his hands upon its head, and confess his sins over it —in effect transferring his guilt to the animal. With the innocent substitute now bearing the guilt, the sinner then slew the animal. Thus the Holy Spirit

106

taught the sinner that forgiveness of sin could be obtained only through confession of guilt and acceptance of the death of a substitute. (Hebrews 9:22.)

But no animal could possibly bear sin. Paul emphatically declared, "It is not possible that the blood of bulls and of goats should take away sins." Hebrews 10:4. The animal served only as a symbol or representative of a far better Substitute, even the Lamb of God. (John 1:29.) By looking forward in faith to the death of Christ, the worshiper realized forgiveness of sin. At the altar the penitent obtained justification by faith. He was free, not to keep on sinning, but free from his guilt. He had the inner assurance of the Holy Spirit that God would provide a complete atonement for his sin. Thus the brazen altar pointed clearly to Christ's substitutionary death.

God made forgiveness conditional upon future obedience. "When I shall say to the righteous, that he shall surely live; if he trust to his own righteousness and commit iniquity, all his righteousnesses shall not be remembered; but for his iniquity that he hath committed, he shall die for it." Ezekiel 33:13. The heart of God calls after the erring, "Turn, O backsliding children, saith the Lord; for I am married unto you." "Return, ye backsliding children, and I will heal your backslidings." Jeremiah 3:14, 22. "As I live, saith the Lord God, I have no pleasure in the death of the wicked; . . . turn ye, turn ye from your evil ways; for why will ye die, O house of Israel?" Ezekiel 33:11. At the altar God offers forgiveness for every repentant sinner. But God will not be imposed upon. He offers mercy only to those who confess and forsake their sins. (Proverbs 28:13.)

Here at the altar the Holy Spirit revealed the mystery of the amazing love that reconciles repentant sinners. "For God so loved the world, that he gave his only begotten Son" to be man's substitute, to carry his guilt to the cross, and to die there in his place, "that whosoever believeth in him should not perish," but be entirely reconciled to God and receive eternal life. (John 3:16.)

The Holy Place: The two apartments of the sanctuary explain how God handles confessed sin and opens the way to His throne.

Morning and evening throughout the year the priests offered sacrifices at the brazen altar. This was called the daily (also called "continual" or "perpetual") sacrifice. Individual worshipers could not go beyond the altar. But the priest as their go-between, or advocate, ministered the spilled blood in their behalf by taking it into the holy place and sprinkling it there. Though the worshipers could not go into the holy place in person, they were to enter by faith and to expect help to come to them from there. The psalmist prayed, "Send thee help from the sanctuary." Psalm 20:2. What the Old Testament worshiper had in symbol the New Testament believer has in reality. Every type or prophetic representation has an antitype or prophetic fulfillment.

After the crucifixion the Jerusalem Temple be-

108

came desolate. (Matthew 23:38.) After His ascension, Jesus began His High Priestly ministry in the holy place of the heavenly sanctuary. He ministered in this apartment until the antitypical Day of Atonement, the time of the judgment. As Mediator Christ sends the Holy Spirit to impart the divine nature to those who will become new creatures. Not merely does the divine nature influence the human, but it unites with it. (2 Corinthians 5:17; Romans 8:11.)

This new birth produces an infant, not an adult. Just as an infant grows, the Christian is to "grow up into him in all things." (Ephesians 4:15.) "That he no longer should live the rest of his time in the flesh, . . . but to the will of God," and that means to "live according to God in the spirit." (1 Peter 4:2, 6.) "For if ye live after the flesh, ye shall die: but if ye through the Spirit do mortify the deeds of the body, ye shall live." Romans 8:13. God expects the experience of His sons and daughters to be continuous and progressive: "Till we all come . . . unto a perfect man, unto the measure of the stature of the fulness of Christ." Ephesians 4:13. The holy place and the activities associated with it portray the new creature in Christ Jesus as he develops a fitness for heaven and advances in sanctification.

Many begin their Christian warfare very bravely but fail to reckon with their natural tendencies to evil, and in a moment of weakness they stumble. But even though they have done wrong, they should not be discouraged. The beloved apostle wrote, "My little children, these things write I unto you, that ye sin not. And if any man sin, we have an advocate with the Father, Jesus Christ the righteous." 1 John 2:1. The writer of Hebrews observes, "We have a great high priest, that is passed into the heavens." "Let us therefore come boldly unto the throne of grace, that we may obtain mercy, and find grace to help in time of need." Hebrews 4:14, 16.

Whom God forgives He places on probation to develop a Christlike character. He may make mistakes, yet in answer to his prayer, Jesus, his Mediator, will intercede for him, obtain forgiveness for him, and send the Holy Spirit to help him overcome. The plan of salvation would be incomplete without the services of our divine Mediator.

In the first apartment where the daily ministration takes place God treats each case sympathetically. All may have the experience of Paul in dying to self daily and in receiving the daily benefits of Christ's mediation. (1 Corinthians 15:31; Galatians 2:20.) All who would grow in the Holy Spirit must obtain help each day. The services in the holy place do not teach that once forgiven one will never sin again or that once saved means always saved. (1 John 1:8, 9.)

The holy place reveals a peculiar type of love— an affectionate love born of pity—long-suffering, wooing, yearning courtship love that refuses to be offended by the mistakes of the one loved but willingly provides for every struggler toward the kingdom a Mediator who is able "to save them to the uttermost that come unto God by him, seeing he ever liveth to make intercession for them." (Hebrews 7:25.)

The Most Holy Place: At the end of each year the high priest went alone into the holy of holies to make a special atonement for Israel and to cleanse the sanctuary of the sins that had been transferred there by prayer. (Leviticus 16:29-34.) The ceremonies on the Day of Atonement typified and pointed forward to the day-of-judgment services which would be held in heaven's most holy place. (Daniel 7: 9, 10.)

Paul standing before Felix pointed forward to "judgment to come" (Acts 24:25), and to the Athenians he declared, "He [God] hath appointed a day, in the which he will judge the world in righteousness by that man whom he hath ordained." Acts 17:31. "That man," of course, is Jesus. In the judgment everything depends upon what Jesus means to each Christian personally. Daniel said that he saw, following the judgment, "the Son of man . . . given . . . a kingdom, that all people, nations, and languages, should serve him." (Daniel 7:13, 14.) Prophecy fulfilled and fulfilling tells us that we live near the close of the antitypical Day of Atonement, the time that just precedes Christ's coming as King of kings and Lord of lords. Thus the message "The hour of his judgment is come" (Revelation 14:6, 7) has a special application now.

Every case is now being reviewed in the most

holy place of the heavenly sanctuary. The life history
of every soul who has professed Christ at some time
in his life will be investigated. The mind of every
heavenly intelligence must be satisfied with the fitness of each person for heaven. God will apportion
rewards not only on the basis of what has been done
during the brief span of the life lived in this world
but also upon the influence or fruitage of that life as
it has affected others for good or evil to the very
close of time. (Revelation 14:13.)

Now is the time to heed Peter's admonition, "Repent ye, . . . and be converted, that your sins may be
blotted out, when the times of refreshing [the latter
rain] shall come from the presence of the Lord."
Acts 3:19. Those who fail to have their sins blotted
out will have their names blotted out of the book of
life. (Revelation 3:5.) When every case is settled,
Christ will pronounce the irrevocable verdict, "He
that is unjust, let him be unjust still: . . . and he that
is righteous, let him be righteous still." Revelation
22:11.

As the early rain fell upon the disciples as a result
of Christ's mediation in the holy place, so we may expect the latter rain to fall upon God's commandment-
keeping remnant through His mediation in the most
holy place.

God required the children of Israel to afflict their
souls on the Day of Atonement. (Leviticus 16:29.)
Every sin was to be searched out and confessed, for
only the record of confessed sins, those transferred to

the sanctuary, could be cleansed, or removed, from the most holy place. Sins that had not been transferred to the sanctuary stayed with their perpetrator. God will have a clean universe. "For whatsoever soul it be that shall not be afflicted in that same day, he shall be cut off from among his people." Leviticus 23:29. The self-examination called for anciently will be repeated under the searching influence of "the spirit of judgment" and "the spirit of burning." (Isaiah 4:4.) Where we spend eternity depends upon our dealing truly with our own souls—there will be no future probation. Sin must be overcome while Jesus still mediates. Urgency calls for an immediate heart response.

In the most holy place God reveals His marvelous love, a love which unites justice and mercy, the law and the gospel. This love is "abundant in goodness and truth, . . . forgiving iniquity and transgression and sin," but it "will by no means clear the guilty." (Exodus 34:6, 7.) No one will be lost who wanted to be saved—no one saved who chose to be lost. "For he shall have judgment without mercy, that hath shewed no mercy; and mercy rejoiceth against judgment." James 2:13. The words of the wise man apply here: "He that sinneth against me wrongeth his own soul: all they that hate me love death." Proverbs 8:36.

Only the Holy Spirit can help us to appreciate the inner secrets of the sanctuary. By the Holy Spirit we grasp the central truth that "justice and judgment are the habitation of thy throne," that there, in the most

8   113

holy place, where God sits on His throne, all the problems of man's salvation are solved and resolved. "Mercy and truth are met together; righteousness and peace have kissed each other." (Psalms 89:14; 85:10.)

The Temple Being Built
by the Spirit

"Christ . . . loved the church, and gave himself for it." He intends to "present it to himself a glorious church, not having spot, or wrinkle, or any such thing; but that it should be holy and without blemish." (Ephesians 5:25, 27.) The word *church* as used in the Bible does not refer to a building in which people worship. It rather signifies those who have gathered together. The Christian church consists of those who have in response to the voice of the Holy Spirit found repentance and have experienced conversion, those who have been led by the Spirit to forsake the world and live the new life in Christ Jesus, and those who have been born again by water and the Spirit. (John 3:5.) Christ bestows His su-

preme regard upon His church, for it is "the church
. . . which he hath purchased with his own blood."
(Acts 20:28.)

The church represents God in this world. She
deals with matters of the soul, moral worth, virtuous
living, the higher life, the pure, noble, holy, and true.
Her concerns include worship, the extension of
Christ's spiritual kingdom, and the Bible code of
ethics. She teaches that man empowered by the Spirit
can live in "this present evil world" as he will live
in the new earth.

Isaiah described the church as a watered garden
whose waters fail not. "Water" symbolizes the blessings imparted by the Holy Spirit. (Isaiah 58:11;
44:3.) Paul likened the church to the body of Christ
(Ephesians 1:22, 23), the members of which are
perfectly joined together in love—beautiful symbol
of how the Holy Spirit unifies the activities of church
members so that they act together as one (Ephesians
4:16). The inner secret of the unity of the believers
is that they all partake of "the same Spirit." (1 Corinthians 12:1-13.)

Those born into the family of God think of their
church home as their spiritual home—a home where
all the members of God's family, old and young, rich
and poor, healthy and sick, are treated as they have
need in the daily ministrations. (Acts 6:1-7.) Under
the superintendence of the Holy Spirit the church will
always have overflow blessings to impart to those
nearby and afar off.

116

One of the most vibrant and meaningful symbols which the New Testament applies to the church is the temple. Who is the builder of this spiritual temple? The Holy Spirit. "Ye . . . are built upon the foundation of the apostles and prophets, Jesus Christ himself being the chief corner stone; . . . in whom ye also are builded together for an habitation of God through the Spirit." Ephesians 2:19-22.

Of what material is this spiritual church built? The Apostle Peter portrays the Christian as a living stone in God's spiritual house. (1 Peter 2:5.) To be living stones, we must be infilled with the Spirit of life. (Romans 8:2.) Every person who is indwelt by the Spirit is a spiritual temple in a special sense. "What? know ye not that your body is the temple of the Holy Ghost which is in you, which ye have of God, and ye are not your own? For ye are bought with a price: therefore glorify God in your body, and in your spirit, which are God's." 1 Corinthians 6:19, 20. We should not defile this body temple. Those who abuse the body by wrong habits of eating and drinking, by sensuality (Jude 19), or by excess of any kind pollute this blood-bought temple and call down the wrath of God upon their heads. God's Spirit will not dwell in a defiled temple. (1 Corinthians 3:16, 17.)

God's great spiritual temple consists of many, many living stones; some are pillars in His temple (Revelation 3:12), and some are "corner stones, polished after the similitude of a palace" (Psalm 144:

117

12). Although each person is a living temple, when all are "fitly framed together," they compose God's great temple, His church. (Ephesians 2:21.)

The apostles (that is, the writers of the New Testament) and the prophets (that is, the writers of the Old Testament) make up the foundation of God's great spiritual temple, while Jesus Christ stands as the "elect," "precious," and "chief corner stone." (Ephesians 2:20-22; 1 Peter 2:6.)

The church has had a sorry, and in some cases a stained and spotted, history. It has been disgraced by the inconsistencies of many of its professed members. It has been driven by persecution into many a wilderness exile. It has been attacked on all sides by false teachers, false preachers, false prophets. Undermining from within has added to its trials. False messiahs have plagued its borders.

Yet through it all the church has demonstrated a marvelous vitality. What secret has enabled it to survive so much tribulation and yet extend the triumphs of the cross? It is the inner strength that Christ provided for each member in the gift of the Holy Spirit. No wonder Jesus, looking across the centuries, insisted that the gates of hell would not prevail against her. (Matthew 16:16-18.)

The church's secret of strength consists not in its institutions, its wealth, its pulpit oratory, its well-appointed places of worship, but in the indwelling of the Holy Spirit in the hearts of its members. Those who compose the church when Jesus comes the second time will be those in whom He has put His Spirit and who in their lives have developed the fruits of the Spirit. Those will be but a part of the ransomed of all ages who have lived up to all the light they had. (Proverbs 4:18; 24:12.) Today, in all lands and in all communions, honest-hearted souls are responding to the promptings of the Holy Spirit and living up to all the light that falls upon their path. All such who have accepted Christ are a part of His church and are accepted by the Father. (2 Timothy 2:19.)

The hour for the church to receive power for her militant warfare has arrived. God's temple is to be fully built up. The description found in Song of Solomon 6:10 will soon become a glorious reality: "Who is she that looketh forth as the morning, fair as the moon, clear as the sun, and terrible as an army with banners?"

But before her triumph the church must engage the powers of darkness in a warfare that will bring the warriors of the cross to the very gates of hell. The honest-hearted in all lands and in all communions must be gathered out. The crisis of crises rushes toward us. Christ assures victory, but only through the omnipotent power of the Holy Spirit. The church must now seek that power.

Sealed With
the Holy Spirit

"Our gospel came not unto you in word only, but also in power, and in the Holy Ghost, and in much assurance." 1 Thessalonians 1:5. The "much assurance" given the believer concerns his present and his future. God assures the believer (1) that he is now a child of God, (2) that everlasting life will be his at Christ's return, and (3) that he will have an inheritance in the new earth.

How may one who has surrendered his life to Christ find assurance that God will continue to recognize him as His child? The Bible promises that he who has "heard" the Word of God and "believed" its promises is "sealed with that holy Spirit of promise, . . . the earnest of our inheritance." (Ephesians

1:13, 14.) The presence of the Holy Spirit in the life attests our acceptance. (1 John 3:24; 4:13.) The gift of God's Spirit constitutes the "earnest," or "down payment," which God gives every born-again soul to assure him that the rest of the blessings promised will be given him in due time. And this presence of the Holy Spirit influencing the inner life thus seals or certifies God's promises.

Paul said, "Grieve not the holy Spirit of God, whereby ye are sealed unto the day of redemption." Ephesians 4:30. This "day of redemption" occurs at Christ's coming. Thus the Spirit's presence in the life assures us of a resurrection. (Romans 8:23; Luke 21:27, 28; 1 Thessalonians 4:16, 17.)

Though we cannot comprehend it, God has bequeathed all of His vast holdings to His children. The children of the resurrection are to be "heirs of God, and joint-heirs with Christ." (Romans 8:17.) But how can we know that we shall have an inheritance in the new earth? Paul declared that those who "have the firstfruits of the Spirit" will have the assurance. (Verse 23.) All who have received the Holy Spirit have the initial installment, or binding down payment. With Abraham they can look with confidence for that "city . . . whose builder and maker is God." (Hebrews 11:10-16.)

A seal has many functions. First of all, it produces an image. Whatever is sealed becomes a counterpart of the seal. Job's imagery, "turned as clay to the seal" (Job 38:14), well portrays this aspect of a

121

seal. God has indeed sealed the Christian who reflects the image of Jesus.

A seal also constitutes an announcement that every condition has been met and approved. Of Jesus we read, "Him hath God the Father sealed." John 6:27. Jesus was indeed "approved of God." (Acts 2:22.) Peter described Him as He "who did no sin, neither was guile found in his mouth." (1 Peter 2:22.)

The Bible uses various terms to describe different aspects of the Christian's relationship to heavenly citizenship. The concept of being "sealed" (Ephesians 1:13) looks forward to a finished work; "adoption" (Galatians 4:4-6) emphasizes a relationship; and sanctification (1 Corinthians 6:11) connotes a process. All refer to a progressive experience continuing throughout life.

Christ explained who will be saved: "He that shall endure unto the end, the same shall be saved." Matthew 24:13. "Be thou faithful unto death, and I will give thee a crown of life." Revelation 2:10. Death concludes or seals one's character development. What a man is at death, he will be in the resurrection.

But some living in time's last hour will not come under the power of the grave. They will live to see Jesus come and be "caught up"—that is, translated —at His glorious appearing. (1 Thessalonians 4:16, 17.) The Bible speaks of these as "sealed," not sealed in the grave, but sealed during their lifetime, sealed when probation closes, sealed because in character they have made the necessary preparation to endure the tests and trials of the seven last plagues and meet Christ at His return. But sin can never be approved of God. No one who is not living up to all the light he has will be sealed. (James 4:17.)

Life bears many uncertainties. No one knows what tomorrow holds. But we can know today that we have accepted Christ and that we are accepted by Him because we have the presence of His Spirit in our hearts and lives. We can know today that we are living up to all the light that is falling on our pathway. We can know today that we are settling into the truth through obedience to the Word of God and the Spirit's promptings. We can know that we are day by day being sealed by the Spirit into an experience that will prepare us for Christ's return and qualify us to receive an inheritance in God's everlasting kingdom.

The Latter Rain
Outpouring of the Spirit

It's going to rain. The Bible is no hit-or-miss weather prophet. When the Bible predicts "rain," it will come. The Bible predicts two rains, a rain of "powder and dust" (Deuteronomy 28:24), and "showers of blessing" (Ezekiel 34:26). The first rain the impenitent will receive; the second, the penitent.

The barometer of the Bible pictures stormy times ahead. Of ancient Babylon, Jeremiah declared, "Thus saith the Lord of hosts, Behold, evil shall go forth from nation to nation, and a great whirlwind shall be raised up from the coasts of the earth." And again we read, "Behold, the whirlwind of the Lord goeth forth with fury, a continuing whirlwind: it shall fall with pain upon the head of the wicked. . . . In the latter days ye shall consider it." Jeremiah 25: 32; 30:23, 24. And with this latter-day whirlwind, which vents its fury upon the wicked, will come a strange kind of rain. "Thy heaven that is over thy head shall be brass, and the earth that is under thee shall be iron. The Lord shall make the rain of thy land *powder and dust*." Deuteronomy 28:23, 24. Such will be the lot of men today who harden their hearts against God's Spirit. "A prudent man foreseeth the evil, and hideth himself: but the simple pass on, and are punished." Proverbs 22:3.

But another kind of wind will also blow, the fresh winds of the Holy Spirit; another kind of rain, the latter rain outpouring of the Spirit; and another kind of harvest, the ripened fruit of a mature Christian experience. (Isaiah 4:2.)

"The everlasting gospel" is going with accelerated momentum "to every nation, and kindred, and tongue, and people." (Revelation 14:6, 7.) God has set His hand a "second time" to gather a remnant from the earth. (Isaiah 11:11, 12.) When God sets His hand to do a work, it will be done. "For he will finish the work, and cut it short in righteousness: because a short work will the Lord make upon the earth." Romans 9:28.

The thrilling climax of the plan of salvation lies just ahead when the whole earth will be lighted with God's glory. (Revelation 18:1, 2.) In Moses' day God insisted, "As truly as I live, all the earth shall be filled with the glory of the Lord." Numbers 14:21. Isaiah, though he foresaw a moral blackout in time's last hour—also saw an awakening: "Arise, shine; for thy light is come, and the glory of the Lord is risen upon thee. For, behold, the darkness shall cover the earth, and gross darkness the people: but the Lord shall arise upon thee, and his glory shall be seen upon thee." Isaiah 60:1, 2.

What prerequisites must the church meet in order to receive the outpouring of the Holy Spirit, which will make manifest the glory of the Lord? The fullness of the Holy Spirit will come only after we have had an "upper room" experience similar to that of the disciples of Christ after His resurrection. (Acts 1; 2.) Then we shall emphasize:

Revival and Reformation: Revival calls for a turning from those worldly pursuits that displease God—a conscientious about-face to make God first in all things. God cannot give His Spirit in large measure to lukewarm people who are under the illusion that they are rich and have need of nothing.

Sin cannot be palliated, ignored, or excused. With contrition of heart, all must individually seek the hidden causes of their spiritual feebleness—such as pride of opinion, sensitiveness to slights, unholy ambitions, soul-and-body-destroying lusts, and selfishness in its varied forms—and literally root them out of their lives. The repentance called for in Revelation 3:14-20 must be complete. We must loathe and despise our inconsistencies, our petty feudings, and our involvements with worldly amusements. With warmth and ardor and a holy animation we will testify to the saving grace of Christ.

Christ Our Righteousness: Instead of taking pride in personal attainments, seeking position, place, or power, the heart yearning of everyone will be to exalt and extol the blessed Saviour as the One altogether lovely. When God's people truly glorify Christ, rivers of water will flow from them to bless all whom they contact. (John 7:37-39.)

The theme *righteousness by faith* will no longer be only a formal confession of faith. People will glow with the living experience that has brought them into intimate relationship with Jesus. They will detest the unclean garment of their own righteousness (Isaiah 64:6) and array themselves in the beautiful clothing of heaven (Isaiah 61:10). And as they "sow . . . in righteousness," Jesus will "come and rain righteousness" upon them. (Hosea 10:12.)

Prayer: As earnest, prevailing prayer ascends to the glory courts, we may expect to receive the "latter rain." (Luke 11:13.) Those who do not pray for this blessing disqualify themselves to receive it, for they would not appreciate the gift if God bestowed it upon them. To encourage our petitions, God offers to pour upon His faithful people "the spirit of grace and of supplications." (Zechariah 12:10.) He admonishes, "Ask ye of the Lord rain in the time of the latter rain," and then He promises, "so the Lord shall make bright clouds, and give them showers of rain, to

127

every one grass in the field." Zechariah 10:1. God would have His people eager to receive the blessing He would give them to empower them to reveal the gospel to the whole world.

"Spare Thy People": Specifically the entire church should pray, "Spare thy people, O Lord, and give not thine heritage to reproach." Joel 2:17. The ungodly have ridiculed, mocked, and derided the people of God because their lives did not harmonize with their high profession. The fruits of the Spirit so beautifully exemplified in the life of Jesus are yet to be seen in their fullness in the lives of His children. When in their distress God's people plead for victory and persist until they get victory, the rain will come. (Verse 23.)

Bible Study: Part of the "restitution of all things, which God hath spoken by the mouth of all his holy prophets since the world began" is the "refreshing" spoken of in Acts 3:19-21. When God's people know a fullness of truth through their study of God's Book of Truth, God will give them the "refreshing" promised.

Obedience: "The people in whose heart is my law" (Isaiah 51:7), those who diligently hearken "unto my commandments" (Deuteronomy 11:13, 14), are those who accept the Spirit in faith. "We are his witnesses; . . . and so is also the Holy Ghost, whom God hath given to them that obey him." Acts 5:32. Thus obedience plays a role in the reception of the Spirit.

Perseverance: God has no reluctance to fill His last-day disciples with His Spirit, but in faith (Galatians 3:14) they must follow through in order to receive the blessing. "Then shall we know, if we follow on to know the Lord: his going forth is prepared as the morning; and he shall come unto us as the rain, as the latter and former rain unto the earth." Hosea 6:3. When like Jacob at Jabbok God's last-day disciples wrestle with the angel, saying, "I will not let thee go, except thou bless me," the blessing will come.

Unity: Fellowship of the Spirit produces unity. The Spirit in one disciple could never be at war with the Spirit in another. When the 120 had achieved complete oneness, the Pentecostal showers fell. (Acts 2:1-4.) We may also expect the harvest rain to fall when God's children experience the unity of the Spirit. (Ephesians 4:3-13.) "Thy watchmen shall . . . see eye to eye, when the Lord shall bring again Zion." Isaiah 52:8. This unity of Spirit will unlock the floodgates of spiritual power.

Missionary Witnessing: What message do you have that is so important to the world that you must have the power of the latter rain to tell it? How has that message affected you? What is it doing in you and for you?

Are the three angels' messages of Revelation 14: 6-12, the last messages of mercy to be heralded before Christ's second coming (Revelation 14:14), like a burning fire shut up in your bones so that you feel distressed to remain silent and find relief only in heralding them abroad (Jeremiah 20:9)? The latter rain will fall on those who allow God to use them in any way He chooses.

What can we expect when the latter rain falls? Converts will flock to the church. Zechariah 8:23 predicts, "In those days . . . ten men shall take hold out of all languages of the nations, . . . of him that is a Jew [that is, a believer], saying, We will go with you: for we have heard that God is with you." "The plowman shall overtake the reaper." Amos 9:13.

Converts will not be of the mixed-multitude variety. Isaiah cried out, "Awake, awake, put on thy strength, O Zion: . . . henceforth there shall no more come into thee the uncircumcised and the unclean." Isaiah 52:1. The church waiting for their Lord's return will be "a glorious church, not having spot, or wrinkle, or any such thing." (Ephesians 5:27.) She will be "beautiful" and "comely," "fair as the moon, clear as the sun, and terrible as an army with banners." (Song of Solomon 6:4, 10.)

How will this be accomplished? Will it be by formulas, slogans, and catch phrases? by human wisdom, might, and power? The grand secret of success calls for something more: "Not by might, nor by power, but by my spirit, saith the Lord of hosts." Zechariah 4:6.

Thrilling days lie just ahead. What joy can be compared with that of being used by the Spirit to gather in earth's harvest? "Showers of blessing" await total commitment!

130

Ministers of the Spirit

The gospel will not close in obscurity with only insignificant results. The notable advances of science and the astonishing triumphs of technology will not overshadow it. Man-made earthquakes (underground H-bomb explosions) may cause dishes to rattle and buildings to sway a hundred miles away, but when God arises to shake the earth, the cities of the nations will fall. (Revelation 16:18, 19.) God will more than meet space-age achievements.

God has declared that just preceding those stupendous events which accompany our Saviour's return, He will pour out His Spirit upon all flesh. (Joel 2:28.) God has promised a last-day world-embracing Pentecost. Here and in related Scriptures He has pictured such a turning to God within the church and from without as has not taken place since apostolic days. The everlasting gospel will be proclaimed with more than Pentecostal power "to every nation, and kindred, and tongue, and people." (Revelation 14:6.)

A church-wide revival and reformation must precede the worldwide ministry of the Spirit. As Christ's disciples "continued with one accord in prayer and supplication" (Acts 1:14) in order to receive the outpouring of the Spirit, so in earth's twilight hour the people of God in all lands through "the supply of the Spirit" (Philippians 1:19) will seek "the unity of the Spirit in the bond of peace" (Ephesians 4:3) that will prepare them to receive the promised last-day outpouring.

All who have found unity with the Spirit will find unity in the Spirit with every other Spirit-endued soul. This unity transcends every other, for it stems from love and can exist only among those "having the same love, being of one accord, of one mind." (Philippians 2:1, 2.)

Paul constantly wrote of this unity of spirit, a unity akin to that which exists between the members of the Godhead. For the church at Philippi he prayed that they "stand fast in one spirit, with one mind striving together for the faith of the gospel." (Philippians 1:27.) To the church at Corinth he wrote, "For by one Spirit are we all baptized into one body, . . . and have been all made to drink into one Spirit." 1 Corinthians 12:13.

When the disciples became of one accord in one place, the Pentecostal showers began to fall. (Acts 2:1-4.) Then the 120, filled with the "same love," became "ministers . . . of the spirit" (2 Corinthians 3:6).

All who receive the Spirit are under obligation to share the Spirit. On one occasion the Lord took of the Spirit that was upon Moses and put it upon the seventy elders of Israel. Sixty-eight of the group went to the Tabernacle, where God bestowed His Spirit upon them. Though two had remained in the camp, they still received God's Spirit. Seeing what had happened, Joshua said, "My lord Moses, forbid them." Moses' reply showed the greatness of the man: "Enviest thou for my sake? would God that all the Lord's people were prophets, and that the Lord would put his spirit upon them!" (Numbers 11:25-29.)

Paul had the same concern. Finding disciples in Ephesus, he asked them, "Have ye received the Holy Ghost since ye believed?" Acts 19:2. When this minister of the Spirit learned of their spiritual destitution, he immediately set about to remedy the situation.

But today's church needs to have a new endowment of the Spirit before it can impress a world busied and occupied with its Babel towers of human achievement, its Aladdin lamps and magic carpets, its mansions and skid-row hovels, its racketeers and riots, its political, economic, educational, and social problems. The world refuses to listen to the accounts of how the Spirit used Old Testament prophets and New Testament apostles. The world today pays little heed to those who speak of the religion of our fathers and mothers. The world wants to see what the Spirit can do in the lives of those who profess to serve God now. But where can the world see those who have been signally blessed by the Spirit—where are lives that have been mightily transformed? Where are missionary witnesses charged with the Holy Spirit who are communicating the Spirit to those about them?

Can anything be so frightening as that the sinners in Zion are unafraid? that the hypocrites go unrebuked? that the evil, bold, defiant, and unashamed feel no terror? Conscientious Christians must ask as did Gideon, "Why . . . is all this befallen us? and where be all his miracles which our fathers told us of?" Judges 6:13.

Soon God will wipe away the reproach. The same God that heard the 120 in the upper room will hear His people today and make them ministers of the Spirit. He will give the Spirit not to glorify man, but to glorify Christ. When Christians imbued with the Spirit become living epistles, "known and read of all men," then the sword of the Spirit will be unsheathed and the glories of the cross told abroad. Modern Davids will sing—not to glorify self or glorify music, but to glorify God. Modern Daniels will interpret current events. Nehemiahs will call for Sabbath reform. Then all that the apostles did will be done by every church member. Peters and Pauls and Johns will proclaim Christ's second coming. Then the church will not glory in numbers and statistics, her works of benevolence and mercy, or her institutions and houses of worship; but in the power of the Spirit she will cry to a world going down to destruction, "Save yourselves from this untoward generation." Acts 2:40.

Never has so much been at stake. Many obstacles lie at hand, but the church will meet the greatest challenge of all time, for the world at its worst will see the church at its best. The unity of the believers will be the unity of the Spirit. Missionary witnesses for Christ will make people as conscious of the invisible as they are of the visible. The message of redeeming love will go to every town and hamlet around the world. The heralds of Christ's return will have the courage of the Reformers and the zeal of the evangelists.

Thousands will turn from this sin-drenched world, its follies and foibles, its drunkenness and gluttony, its forms of godliness. A divine compulsion will lead heads of state, merchant princes, the intelligentsia and the lowly, men and women of every walk of life, to step out and willingly make any sacrifice to serve the Prince of peace. "A great company of the priests were obedient to the faith" in the early church. (Acts 6:7.) So among the clergy today many will make the irreversible commitment to become ministers of the Spirit. Church members will face prejudice, persecution, boycott, and even threats of death, but their passion for souls will rise above the fierce opposition of the synagogue of Satan. Indeed, the more desperate the battle, the greater the victory. Satan can do nothing against the truth except what will ultimately result in giving the truth a greater luster.

God wants to use you as a minister of the Spirit in this climax. The whole earth is to be lightened with the glory of the gospel. Language proves inadequate to describe the blending of celestial glory with the bravery of God's last-day witnesses, sealed with the seal of the living God. In vision John beheld their triumph over Satan's final worldwide confederacy of evil. He said, "I saw . . . them that had gotten the victory . . . stand on the sea of glass. . . . And they sing the song of Moses the servant of God, and the song of the Lamb, saying, Great and marvellous are thy works, Lord God Almighty; just and true are thy ways, thou King of saints." Revelation 15:2, 3. Will you join in those mighty hallelujah choruses?

The Sin Against
the Holy Spirit

Above Niagara Falls a place called "Past Redemption Point" marks the spot where the waters quicken and the current becomes so swift that no possibility exists for a person to turn back. Similarly, for those walking in the gilded and glittering broad way there comes a time when the current of evil quickens and nothing can save them. Why? Because they have refused to be impressed by the Holy Spirit so often that they go beyond their soul's "Past Redemption Point."

This is the sin against the Holy Spirit—a sin so irreversible that no future probation for repentance is possible. (Matthew 12:31, 32.) Those who consistently refuse to listen to the voice of God eventually destroy their capacity to hear it.

The appeal of the Spirit heard within the sacred precincts of the soul is called "conviction." Conviction brings the soul under moral obligation to heed and obey. Jesus Himself speaks, saying, "He that hath an ear, let him hear what the Spirit saith unto the churches." Revelation 2:7. Through conviction the Spirit invites us to repent. But repentance or sorrow for sin isn't enough; the soul must turn from sin to Jesus, the Sin Bearer.

Alas, many refuse to heed the pleadings of the Spirit. They treat conviction as an unwelcome annoyance. They "kick against the pricks," attempting to hush the voice of the Spirit, to ignore His promptings, reject His appeals, defy His restraints. Thus man plays the traitor to his soul. Overriding conviction produces presumption. As time goes on, the voice within becomes fainter and fainter until at last it doesn't bother the sinner anymore. Though he "call evil good, and good evil" (Isaiah 5:20), he finds no happiness, only "a certain fearful looking for of judgment and fiery indignation, which shall devour the adversaries" (Hebrews 10:27).

God never gives anyone up. He says, "I will never leave thee, nor forsake thee." Hebrews 13:5. Man forsakes God. Paul describes those who reject God: "Because that, when they knew God, they glorified him not as God, neither were thankful. . . . Wherefore God also gave them up; . . . who changed the truth of God into a lie. . . . For this cause God gave them up. . . . As they did not like to retain God in their knowledge, God gave them over." Romans 1:21-28.

But no Christian should presume to judge who has committed this unpardonable sin, for many, like Paul, who called himself the chief of sinners, have been snatched as a brand from the burning. There are, of course, many who have heeded the voice of the Spirit and in spite of trials and afflictions have followed through to gain notable victories for God.

The eleventh chapter of Hebrews has been called the Bible Hall of Fame. This chapter lists such heroes of faith as Enoch, Noah, Abraham, and Moses. By faith many of the men listed gained victories in situations that some would call defeats: they endured mockings and scourgings and imprisonments. They endured! And that's victory! They endured because they obeyed and kept on obeying the "still small voice" within, doing whatever that voice asked, believing that God would do as He had promised. (Isaiah 3:10.)

But most have taken another course. God says, "I have called, and ye refused; I have stretched out my hand, and no man regarded; but ye have set at nought all my counsel, and would none of my reproof: . . . when distress and anguish cometh upon you; then shall they call upon me, but I will not answer; . . . they despised all my reproof. Therefore shall they eat of the fruit of their own way." Proverbs 1:24-31.

139

Jude referred to these as the "twice dead." "Woe unto them! for they have gone in the way of Cain, and ran greedily after the error of Balaam for reward, and perished in the gainsaying of Core. . . . Clouds they are without water [a symbol of the Holy Spirit]; . . . trees whose fruit withereth, without fruit, twice dead; . . . wandering stars, to whom is reserved the blackness of darkness for ever." Jude 11-13.

The Apostle Paul said, "It is impossible for those who . . . have tasted the good word of God, and the powers of the world to come, if they shall fall away, to renew them again unto repentance." Hebrews 6: 4-6. The bodies of those who have rejected God's Spirit become but corpses. Today many a treacherous Judas betrays his Lord with a kiss, many like Ananias and Sapphira lie to the Holy Spirit, many a covetous Achan troubles Israel, and many a painted Jezebel worships Baal. For them "the harvest is past, the summer is ended, and . . . [they] are not saved." (Jeremiah 8:20.)

When the whole world in Noah's day was about to commit the unpardonable sin, God sent Noah, a preacher of righteousness, to warn them. God declared to that sin-drenched generation, "My spirit shall not always strive with man." Genesis 6:3. This warning has an application today, for "as it was in the days of Noe, so shall it be also in the days of the Son of man." Luke 17:26.

When Lot rushed to his sons-in-law in the dead of night with the warning, "Up, get you out of this place; for the Lord will destroy this city," "he seemed as one that mocked." Genesis 19:14. The Spirit of God had left them. Again: "As it was in the days of Lot; . . . even thus shall it be in the day when the Son of man is revealed." Luke 17:28-30. And when Israel refused repentance, the Lord declared, "Ephraim is joined to idols: let him alone." Hosea 4:17.

The sin against the Holy Ghost is always self-inflicted, and entirely needless—there can be no excuse for it. He who continually disregards the warnings of the Spirit until his soul at last becomes stone-deaf to the voice of entreaty carries full responsibility for his condition since he himself has chosen deafness. The unpardonable sin might be termed spiritual suicide.

The Holy Spirit always has our best interests at heart. He labors with us to help us overcome inbred tendencies and inclinations to sin and battle the evil suggestions and influences of Satan and his angels, "for we wrestle not against flesh and blood, but . . . against wicked spirits." (Ephesians 6:12, margin.) Too often we have failed to recognize the supernatural nature of the struggle in which we are engaged, and we don't realize our inadequacies. The battle for the soul goes on within the soul. To ignore the Spirit's promptings means to reject the divine help Heaven has provided. Soon the world will be divided into two classes: those filled with the Holy Spirit and those filled with an unholy spirit.

Actually the only sin that God cannot forgive is

the sin we refuse to forsake. "He is able also to save them to the uttermost that come unto God by him." Hebrews 7:25. The first work of the Spirit is to plead with the soul to come. "The Spirit and the bride say, Come." Revelation 22:17. To respond to this invitation is the finest thing a man can ever do—to resist, the worst.

The Bible gives several ways in which we might sin against the Holy Spirit.

1. *By refusing to hear the Spirit.* "They refused to hearken, . . . and stopped their ears, that they should not hear. Yea, they made their hearts as an adamant stone, lest they should hear the law, and the words which the Lord of hosts hath sent in his spirit by the former prophets." Zechariah 7:11, 12.

2. *By quenching the Spirit.* "Quench not the Spirit." 1 Thessalonians 5:19.

3. *By grieving the Spirit.* "Grieve not the holy Spirit of God." Ephesians 4:30.

4. *By resisting the Spirit.* "Ye do always resist the Holy Ghost." Acts 7:51.

5. *By vexing the Spirit.* "They rebelled, and vexed his holy Spirit." Isaiah 63:10.

6. *By doing despite to the Spirit.* Hebrews 10:29 speaks of some who did "despite unto the Spirit of grace."

7. *By hardening our hearts against the Spirit.* "The Holy Ghost saith, To day if ye will hear his voice, harden not your hearts." Hebrews 3:7, 8.

But the Christian who loves Jesus, who lives up

to all the light he has, will be in no danger of committing the unpardonable sin as long as he grows "in grace, and in the knowledge of our Lord and Saviour Jesus Christ." (2 Peter 3:18.)

Daily we must reaffirm our past consecrations and renew our past decisions to go all the way with Jesus. "He that shall endure unto the end, the same shall be saved." Matthew 24:13.

"Cast not away therefore your confidence, which hath great recompence of reward. For ye have need of patience, that, after ye have done the will of God, ye might receive the promise. For yet a little while, and he that shall come will come, and will not tarry. Now the just shall live by faith: but if any man draw back, my soul shall have no pleasure in him. But we are not of them who draw back unto perdition; but of them that believe to the saving of the soul." Hebrews 10:35-39.